INCREDIBLE
BASEBALL
STORIES

INCREDIBLE BASEBALL STORIES

STORIES

AMAZING TALES FROM THE DIAMOND

EDITED BY KEN SAMELSON

Skyhorse Publishing

Skyhorse Publishing books may be purchased in bulk at special discounts for sales promotion, corporate gifts, fund-raising, or educational purposes. Special editions can also be created to specifications. For details, contact the Special Sales Department, Skyhorse Publishing, 307 West 36th Street, 11th Floor, New York, NY 10018 or info@skyhorsepublishing.com.

Skyhorse® and Skyhorse Publishing® is are registered trademarks of Skyhorse Publishing, Inc.®, a Delaware corporation.

Visit our website at www.skyhorsepublishing.com.

10 9 8 7 6 5 4 3

Library of Congress Cataloging-in-Publication Data is available on file.

Cover design by Tom Lau
Cover photo credit: AP Images

Print ISBN: 978-1-5107-1381-9
Ebook ISBN: 978-1-5107-1386-4

Printed in the United States

TABLE OF CONTENTS

INTRODUCTION

Ilove reading about baseball. And if you've picked up this book, I'm
sure you do, too. When I first became interested in the sport as a
youngster growing up in the Bronx, I read just about everything
I could about our national pastime—from biographies to team histo-
ries to greatest World Series moments, it didn't really matter. I loved
all sports, but especially baseball. I think I bought just about every
book—and there were many—that was published after the "Miracle
Mets" won the 1969 World Series. But I was not just a provincial fan—I
wanted to stay informed about the entire world of baseball. I read the
sports pages of the *Daily News* and *New York Post* every day, and the
New York Times on Sunday. I subscribed to the *Sporting News*, regularly
visited local newsstands and candy stores to buy baseball magazines,
and read as many baseball books as I could, either purchasing them or
wearing out a path to the public library to borrow them.

The early 1970s were a particularly good time to read about baseball—I learned the art of "beaver shooting" and added many colorful
swear words to my vocabulary from reading Jim Bouton's groundbreaking *Ball Four*, a book I still go back and read from time to time. I

loved books written by the two Rogers, Kahn (*The Boys of Summer*) and Angell (*The Summer Game*). My baseball library now takes up several bookshelves in my crowded apartment, and a signed copy of Lawrence Ritter's classic *The Glory of Their Times* is one of my prized possessions.

The baseball knowledge I gained over the years served me well when I became one of the editors of *The Baseball Encyclopedia*, first published by Macmillan the same year those Mets stunned the baseball world. The "Big Mac" contained career statistics of every player who ever appeared in a major league game dating back to 1871. I worked on the seventh edition, published in 1988, all the way through to the tenth and final edition in 1996. One of the highlights of my time at Macmillan was getting to meet Jim Bouton when we published the twentieth anniversary edition of *Ball Four*. When Bouton found out I worked on *The Baseball Encyclopedia*, he remarked that he finished his major league career a game under .500 (at 62–63) and asked me if there was anything I could do to change it. "I'll make it worth your while," he joked, and we shared a good laugh over that.

Several times during those years, I was approached by people who wanted to know why their grandfather or uncle didn't appear in the book, and I nicely told them I would look into it, but the fact was that they never made it into a big league box score, even if they had played in the minors or spent time in major league camp during spring training. Several major leaguers contacted us to correct information such as their hometown or date of birth. I remember having nice conversations with players such as Allie Reynolds, who wanted us to correct his birthdate. I treasured talking to them, and sometimes they would even share stories about their playing days.

I am reminded about this because a few years ago my parents told me about an acquaintance that had some great stories about playing baseball in the 1950s. While he never made the majors and didn't claim to be in *The Baseball Encyclopedia*, William "Bill" Booth had some great reminiscences about life as a Dodgers farmhand in the late 1950s. He became friendly with Jackie Robinson, shielded Vin Scully from flying baseballs during batting practice, and once while throwing BP nearly beaned Don Zimmer, who had once suffered a fractured skull after being hit in the head with a pitch. We hit it off immediately and struck up a lasting friendship. Now in his late seventies and living in South Florida, where he gives golf lessons and works as an exterminator, he is still a commanding presence at 6-foot-4. We talk about a variety of things including politics and our favorite television shows, but the talk always comes back to baseball. He is fond of saying baseball is your friend because it can keep you company all season long. Bill competes in high-stakes fantasy leagues and always has an opinion about what's going on in baseball from why Bryce Harper might be struggling to whom the Detroit Tigers should use as their closer.

It is amazing the connections you can share through baseball. When Bill found out that I live in Westchester, in the suburbs north of New York City, he recalled pitching a game in Yonkers as a member of the "Brooklyn Dodger Rookies" in the 1950s. He told me that from time to time the Dodger Rookies included a few future major leaguers including Tommy Davis, Bob Aspromonte, and John Orsino. I did some research and found a story in the Yonkers *Herald Statesman* dated August 8, 1956. The game, against a team called the Westchester All-Stars, ended in a 1–1 tie after ten innings. According to the account, "It was a messy game and there were nine errors, seven by the visitors. . . . It was strictly a pitcher's duel between Hal Hitchcock of the hosts . . . and Billy Booth, an eighteen-year-old six-four righty from Scotch Plains, N. J. . . . Booth had to pitch a lot with men on, but he had heart and was quick and effective." The only run Bill surrendered came as the result of an error by the third baseman, a catcher's interference call, and a dropped fly ball by the center fielder. One member of each team was awarded a Most Valuable Player trophy after the game, and "Booth won Brooklyn honors hands down for he had no great help." While reading the story, I was struck by two things. First, the crowd was 2,000 at Fleming Field—the very same park that my son Spencer, a former college player, pitches at several times a season for his semipro team. I don't think more than a dozen people, mostly friends and family members, show up at his games there. Second, the article was written by Bill Libby, who went on to become a prolific author of several sports books, including biographies of Pete Rose, Reggie Jackson, and Catfish Hunter, many of which I had read while growing up!

Of the many stories Bill has shared with me, one of my favorites concerns a certain future Hall of Fame manager, who was a cut-up even back then:

"March 1958 . . . Vero Beach, Florida, Dodgertown, the home of the now Los Angeles Dodgers spring training facility. I was a minor league pitcher under contract to the Dodgers, and on this particular morning I was on my way to a back field to join my teammates assigned to the Green Bay, Wisconsin, Dodgers. The local papers were full of stories about the Dodgers' signing of Frank (Hondo) Howard, a 6'8", 260-pound All-American out of Ohio State. Our manager was Pete Reiser, and we were about to play an intra-organization practice game. I saw a lot of Big Frank for the next few days. Big-time power to say the least. He would loosen up with three bats and a groundskeeper's shovel. The next morning I found out we would be playing a night game against the Montreal Royals at Holman Stadium, and I was scheduled to pitch. Obviously the brass wanted to show off their new player Hondo in front of a big crowd, the media, and everyone in the organization. OK, Frank comes to bat in the second inning, and I struck him out swinging with a change curve. In the fifth, I had a 1–0 lead and here comes Hondo again. We go 3 and 1, and catcher Doug Camilli (son of Dolph) calls for the curve again. I'm thinking that's what Frank is thinking and shook off the curve in favor of high heat. The last time I saw that ball it was disappearing into the moon somewhere over the Atlantic Ocean. It's now 1–1 and I know this is my last inning, so I waited for things to quiet down. A voice from the Montreal dugout was loud and clear: 'Don't worry kid, we'll look for it later!' It was pitcher Tommy Lasorda. I had first met him a year earlier when he came up to me on the mound when I was pitching in a practice game, asked me for the ball, threw one pitch, and then continued walking to the clubhouse with his Montreal teammates, laughing all the way."

The pages that follow include a wide variety of stories that span the entire history of the game, and I hope that reading them adds to your enjoyment and appreciation of our national pastime.

—Ken Samelson, October 2016

PART ONE

THIS GREAT GAME

CHAPTER 1

THE EVOLUTION OF BASEBALL

ALBERT SPALDING

However views of individuals may differ as to the origin of the American national game, all must agree that the sport had as its foundation—a Ball. Without that as its basis, the superstructure of the grandest pastime ever devised by man could never have been erected.

Josh Billings, in writing upon the general subject of Dogs, once said that, in order to realize on the different kinds of dogs, one must have environments calculated to develop the inherent traits of the varied breeds. Thus, in order to "realize" on a coach dog, one must be the owner of a carriage and team, that the canine might run along beneath the vehicle; in order to "realize" on a Newfoundland dog, he said its owner must have a pond of water and children, playing around, carelessly, that they might fall in and be rescued by "Faithful Nero," and so on.

Just so in this case, in order to "realize" on the Ball it is necessary to have someone to put it in motion. Happily, that one is not difficult to find. Placing the Ball in the hands of the first lad who happens along, we may be assured that he will do the rest. And he does. In less time than it takes in the telling, he is bounding the sphere upon the ground. Down it goes; up it flies. Leaving the boy's hand, it strikes the ground, and, returning, is caught. In this completed act we have the first crude and elementary step in our National Game—with just a Boy and a Ball.

But the Boy, like other members of the human family, is a social creature. It is quite conceivable that the average boy, upon being presented with a Ball, would find immediate and pleasurable entertainment throwing it to the ground and catching it upon the rebound; but such pastime would be of temporary duration. The lad would soon tire of the monotony of the sport. Unselfish, he would want someone to share his fun—moreover, everybody recognizes that thing in human nature, in youth as well as maturity, which delights in the exploitation of ownership, possession. Given the boy's mother or sister in possession of a new gown, and it is immediately donned for exhibition before her less favored neighbor. The arrival of his new "Red Devil" sets the boy's dad rushing around town before he knows the first principles of the machine's construction, to the imminent danger of all resident mankind and incidentally that of any animal that may happen to come in his way. He simply *must* show Jones the new flyer, even though it decimates the population.

"Like father, like son." Tom wants his schoolmate, Dick, to see the new ball. In a very few minutes they are together, playing throw and catch, in an interesting elementary game of ball. Tom throws; Dick catches. Dick throws; Tom catches. Back and forth flies the ball till the school bell rings, and in this simple little form of exercise we have "Throw and Catch" as the second stage in the evolution of our game—with Two Boys and a Ball.

Now, human nature is not only social in its demands; it is also enterprising—and fickle. Bounding a ball on the ground is well enough if a lad is alone and can't get company. Throw and Catch beats no game at all; but it becomes tiresome after a while. And so, when school is over, or on Saturdays, when there is no school, we find Tom and Dick out behind the barn, inventing a new and different phase of the game of ball.

"I'll tell you what we'll do," says Tom. "I'll throw the ball against the barn. You get that old axe-handle over there and strike at it as it comes back. If you miss the ball and I catch it, you're out; or, if you hit the ball and can run and touch the barn and return before I can get the ball and hit you with it, you count one. If I hit you with the ball before you get back to your place, you're out. See?"

Two boys with a ball and bat, playing Barn Ball. *From the New York Public Library A.G. Spalding Collection.*

They try it; find it works well, and the third stage of the game is developed in "Barn-Ball"—with Two Boys, a Bat and a Ball.

Again, it happens sometimes that it is not altogether convenient to play barn-ball. The game requires a barn. Now, while most boys may usually be depended upon to have a large and varied assortment of things in pocket, it sometimes occurs that a barn is not one of them; so barn-ball is out of the question. Tom and Dick are coming from school with Harry. They tell the new boy about the ball and the large amount of fun there is wrapped up in it. They dilate upon the proficiency they have already attained in throwing, catching and batting, and patronize Harry a trifle perhaps, because of his inexperience.

"Why can't we have a game of barn-ball, now?" asks the unsophisticated Harry.

"Oh, don't you know nuthin'? There isn't any barn," answers Dick.

"I'll tell you what we can do," says the inventive Tom. "Come on, Dick; you and I will throw and catch, just as we did the other day, and Harry can stand between us with the club. Now, Dick, when I throw to you, Harry can face me and try to hit the ball, and when you throw to me he can turn your way and strike at it. If Harry misses the ball, and either of us catches it before it hits the ground or on the first bound, he's out and the fellow who catches him out takes the club. If he hits the ball far enough to get to that rock over there and back before one of us gets the ball and hits him with it, he counts one tally; but if one of us hits him with the ball, he's out. See?" And thus the game of "One Old Cat" was born, and the fourth step has been evolved, with Three Boys, a Bat, a Ball and a Base.

The evolution of the next step in the game of Base Ball was natural and easy. It was a very simple sequence of One Old Cat. It grew out of the fact that Jim came along and wanted to play with the others.

"That's dead easy," says the resourceful Tom. "We'll just add another base, get another club, and there you are. All the difference there will be is that when either one hits the ball you must both run and exchange places. If the ball is thrown and hits either one of you, that one must give way to the fellow who threw it." The game of Two Old Cat was thus developed in order to include Four Boys, Two Bats, Two Bases and a Ball.

By this time the game of Base Ball is becoming popular. Next Saturday, when Tom, Dick, Harry and Jim go out on the commons to have a game of Two Old Cat, Frank and Ned join them with hopes of getting into the game.

"No use," says the pessimistic Dick; "only four can play at this game. You see, we've got two catchers and two hitters now, and that's all we can have."

"Oh, I don't know," says Tom. "What's the matter with having a three-cornered game? Then we all can play."

The game is tried three-cornered. It works all right, and Three Old Cat, with Six Boys, Three Bats, Three Bases and a Ball has added another step in the evolution of our American game.

The interest increases. Eight Boys want a chance to play at the same time. An equilateral ground is chosen, about forty feet each way. The sport is tried out in that form and is found to meet the purpose. But now the game is becoming cumbersome. It is slow and unsatisfactory in some respects. The multiplication of players introduces elements of discord. Dissensions arise. No two agree as to the proper way of playing the game. There are no printed rules available for the village commons. Interest, meanwhile, is growing, and more and still more players are clamoring for admission. The game of Four Old Cat has been developed all right, but, unlike the feline from which its name has been derived, the game is never a howling success; but it does afford pastime for Eight Boys, Four Bats, Four Bases and a Ball.

In Two, Three and Four Old Cat games, each individual player had his own score, and the players did not engage collectively as teams. Each tally was credited to the striker only. Every base gained by the striker was counted as a tally for himself alone. At the close of the game, if any record was kept, the player who was found to have the greatest number of tallies was declared the victor. Thus, in the days when a game which would accommodate no more than eight players would suffice, the "Old Cat," or "Individual Score," system of ball-playing answered the purpose; but as the pastime became more popular, and more boys wanted to play, it became necessary to devise a new form of the game which would admit a greater number of participants and at the same time introduce the competitive spirit that prevails in teamwork.

We are indebted to Four Old Cat for the square-shaped ball field, with a base at each corner. A natural step was then made by eliminating the four throwers and four batters of the Four Old Cat game, and substituting in place of them one thrower, or pitcher, and one batter. The pitcher was stationed in the center of the square and the striker, or batter, had his position at the middle of one of the sides of the square. In this form of the game, two sides, or teams, were chosen, one known as the Fielding Side, and the other as the Batting Side. The game was known as "Town Ball," and later, that is, in the decade beginning with 1850, it came to be known as the "Massachusetts Game of Base Ball," in contradistinction to the "New York Game of Base Ball," as played by the Knickerbocker Club of New York City in the decade of the '40s. Thus Town Ball came in vogue and made another step in the evolution of the American game of Base Ball.

Thirty or more players (15 or more on each side) with a bat and ball playing Town Ball. *From the New York Public Library A.G. Spalding Collection.*

In this game were present many of the elements of the game of Base Ball as we know it to-day—and then some. It accommodated thirty or more players and was played on town-meeting days, when everybody in the township took a hand. Sometimes there were so many playing that the grounds were full of fielders, and but for the large number and their indiscriminate selection, the sport might have developed more skill. The square field of Four Old Cat, but with the side lines lengthened to sixty instead of forty feet, obtained in Town Ball. Batsmen were out on balls caught on fly or first bound, and base runners were out by being "soaked" while running by a thrown ball. Town Ball was played quite generally throughout New England. It had, as before stated, fifteen or more players on a side, Catcher, Thrower, Four Bases, a Bat and a Ball.

The final step in the evolution of the game was the adoption of the diamond-shaped field and other points of play incorporated in the system devised by Abner Doubleday, of Cooperstown, New York, in

1839, and subsequently formulated into a code of playing rules adopted by the Knickerbocker Base Ball Club, of New York, upon its organization in 1845. The number of players participating in a game was limited to eighteen—nine on a side; a Pitcher, a Catcher, a Short Stop, First, Second and Third Basemen, Right, Center, and Left Fielders, Four Bases, Bat and Ball, and was the game of Base Ball substantially as played to-day.

The following, from the *Memphis Appeal*, of date unknown to the writer, is a fair and interesting description of the game as played in the days of long ago:

"Time will not turn backward in his flight, but the mind can travel back to the days before Base Ball, or at least to the days before Base Ball was so well known and before it had become so scientific. There were ball games in those days, in town and country, and the country ball game was an event. There were no clubs. The country boy of those days was not gregarious. He preferred flocking by himself and remaining independent. On Saturday afternoons the neighborhood boys met on some well cropped pasture, and whether ten or forty, every one was to take part in the game. Self-appointed leaders divided the boys into two companies by alternately picking one until the supply was exhausted. The bat, which was no round stick, such as is now used, but a stout paddle, with a blade two inches thick and four inches wide, with a convenient handle dressed onto it, was the chosen arbiter. One of the leaders spat on one side of the bat, which was honestly called 'the paddle,' and asked the leader of the opposition forces. 'Wet, or dry?' The paddle was then sent whirling up into the air, and when it came down, whichever side won went to the bat, while the others scattered over the field. The ball was not what would be called a National League ball, nowadays, but it served every purpose. It was usually made on the spot by some boy offering up his woolen socks as an oblation, and these were raveled and wound round a bullet, a handful of strips cut from a rubber overshoe, a piece of cork or almost anything, or nothing, when anything was not available. The winding of this ball was an art, and whoever could excel in this art was looked upon as a superior being. The ball must be a perfect sphere and the threads as regularly laid as the wire on a helix of a magnetic armature. When the winding was complete the surface of the ball was thoroughly sewed with a large needle and thread to prevent it from unwinding when a thread was cut. The diamond was not arbitrarily marked off as now. Sometimes there were four bases, and sometimes six or seven. They were not equidistant, but were marked by, any fortuitous rock, or shrub, or depression in the ground where the steers were wont to bellow and paw up the earth. One of these tellural cavities was almost sure to be selected as 'the den,' now called the home-plate. There were no masks, or mitts, or protectors. There was no science or chicanery, now called 'head-work.' The strapping young oafs—embryonic preachers, presidents and premiers—were too honest for this. The pitcher was the one who could throw the ball over the 'den,' and few could do this. His object was to throw a ball that could be hit. The paddle man's object was to hit the ball, and if he struck at it—which he need not do unless he chose—and missed it, the catcher, standing well back, tried to catch it after it had lost its momentum by striking the earth once and bounding in the air—'on the first bounce' it was called—and if he succeeded the paddleman was dead and another took his place. If he struck it and it was not caught in the field or elsewhere, in the air or on the first bounce, he could strike twice more, but the third time he was compelled to run. There was no umpire, and very little wrangling. There was no effort to pounce upon a base runner and touch him with the ball. Anyone having the ball could throw it at him, and if it hit him he was 'dead'—almost literally sometimes. If he dodged the ball, he kept on running till the den was reached. Some of the players became proficient in ducking, dodging and sidestepping, and others learned to throw the ball with the accuracy of a rifle bullet. No matter how many players were on a side, each and every one had to be put out. And if the last one made three successive home runs, he 'brought in his side,' and the outfielders, pitcher and catcher had to do their work all over again. The boy who could bring in his side was a hero. No victorious general was ever prouder or more lauded. Horatius at the bridge was small potatoes in comparison. He was the uncrowned king. There were no foul hits. If the ball touched the bat ever so lightly it was a 'tick,' and three ticks meant a compulsory run. The score was kept by some one cutting notches in a stick, and the runs in an afternoon ran up into the hundreds. If a ball was lost in the grass or rolled under a Scotch thistle, the cry 'lost ball' was raised and the game stopped until it was found.

"Only the older country ball players can remember those days and games. They did not last long. When the change came, it came suddenly. Technicalities and rules began to creep in. Tricks between the pitcher and catcher, designed to fool the batter, began. The argot or slang of the game intruded. The country boys who went to college found more than their new homespun suits, of which they were so proud on leaving home, out of date. The ball game was all changed. They had to use a round club instead of a paddle to hit the ball. They had to change their tactics all through the game. They found the pitcher not intent upon throwing a ball that could be hit, but so that it would be hit at and missed. The bases were laid off with mathematical accuracy. They could be put out in many unknown and surprising ways. They could not throw a ball at a base runner. They could not wander at will over the field, but must occupy a certain position. All was changed. All has been changed since. The expert of even twenty years ago would be lost to-day. The game of ball has been growing more scientific every year. It will continue to grow more scientific for years to come. The homespun-clad boys who returned home on vacation expecting to 'show off,' and teach their former companions the game of ball up to date, discovered the innovation had preceded them, and that those who had not left the old haunts knew all about the game excepting the very newest wrinkles. And they knew something which the college boys had not learned."

CHAPTER 2

TEAM WORK

JOHN MCGRAW

Various estimates have been hazarded by experts on the value of a manager to a ball club. Some critics do not figure him into the equation at all, while others overrate him. It is a co-operative position. The team cannot get along without a directing force, and the manager cannot succeed without a team. In these remarks on managing a team, in the case of most amateur clubs they will apply to the captain when I refer to the duties of the manager, because, as a rule, such a club does not have any other leader.

Team play is very important to the success of a club, and it is increasing in its importance every season. Within the last three years I have seen clubs in the Big Leagues composed of good players which have failed to succeed because they lacked an efficient style of team play.

First, if you are the captain or manager of a ball club, select your general style of play. If you have a team of fast men, I would advise the shifting, versatile attack, switching constantly on your opponents.

This keeps them guessing, and the great thing to do is to worry your enemies on the diamond.

If the club is slow and inclined to be sluggish, but has many hard hitters, you will have to adopt a more conservative plan. It is foolish to send a slow man down to steal second. You will be forced to depend on the batting of the men who follow him to the plate. Players of the sluggish cast are not so desirable as the other type. Speed is the great thing nowadays.

Never let the other side see you are beaten or are losing courage. *Photo by Lena Samelson.*

Keep after the players all the time. Encourage them and insist that they keep constantly on their toes. Make them show plenty of pepper and spirit and aggression. This carries a long way. Never let the other side see you are beaten or are losing courage.

First of all, the young ball player must learn about the "stages" of a game. There are many things you would try at one "stage" which would be ridiculous under other conditions. There are times when it pays to be conservative and others when it is best to take the long chance. The latter represents the desperate "stage." Every team should have a leader in charge, whether he is the captain or manager, and the players should obey his orders implicitly. If he is not competent, get another leader, but follow the man you have picked out.

Players make a hit with me who work hard all the time, show an aggressive spirit, and keep chewing the rag. As long as an infield maintains a running fire of conversation, the other team is impressed with your confidence. It also keeps up the fighting spirit of your fellow-players. Now, do not misunderstand me by the use of the term "fighting spirit."

There is such a thing in a ball game as a healthy, fighting spirit that does not necessitate a knowledge of the Marquis of Queensberry rules and regulations. Keep after the other team all the time by every fair means you have at your command. It's all right to try to discourage an opponent by clean conversation.

"We'll get you yet," you can shout at him if you are behind. "Watch us come at the finish."

Or if your club is leading:

"We'll, we've got you on the run. You'll never catch us now."

The young player must remember that it is best to sacrifice individual records for the team success. Always play for the club first. And

Young players should sacrifice individual records for team success. *Photo by Bill Winn, courtesy of Albert Arana.*

while we are still discussing the spirit of a club, which comes under the head of team work, I want to advise all infielders to throw the ball around as much as possible when no danger is attached to the process. If a runner is retired at first and there are no others on the bases, pass the ball around the infield with a display of pepper that would look like a show of confidence on a moving-picture film. It impresses the other team, and, besides, keeps the infielders, who may have been idle for some time, livened up and warmed to their work. But always be careful not to throw the ball around if there is a man on base, when a wild heave would be detrimental to your club. Bear in mind constantly the "stage" of the game, which means keeping track of the number of outs in the inning, the score, and the count on the batter.

Roughly speaking, we will consider two "stages," although the game is subdivided into many more by the smart Big League manager. One "stage" is when the score is close, and the other when a large margin separates the two opposing clubs. If the score is close and your club is leading by a single run, say, you must take every chance to add to this lead so you will be safer. One run is of immense value to your team then. It will double your lead. Play what we Big Leaguers call a close game.

Suppose the first batter in the inning gets on base. Order the next hitter to sacrifice so the first one can reach second, from where a hit will score him. You are figuring on the other side playing the game cleanly in laying your plans this way. Baseball is largely a matter of chance and probability, and it is the man who can figure the chances closest and get the right answer the greatest number of times who is the best leader. If you advance the runner to second, he has two chances of scoring on a clean hit because there is only one out when he reaches the middle station.

Besides these chances on a clean hit, there is always the possibility of an error which may break up the game. Seasoned players will tell you that more errors are made on a bunt than on any other kind of a ball. The bunt must be handled hastily and accurately. Therefore, when the batter is instructed to sacrifice, which means bunting, there is the chance of the runner reaching third or scoring on a fumble or bad throw. He is sure of second. A lead of two runs is fairly safe in the Big League, because then you have time to see a storm coming and yank your pitcher before the score is tied.

But if circumstances have convinced you that the bunt is not the play at this time because the opposing club is looking for it, or for some other reason, you might try the hit and run. This is a more open game and has been worked successfully by my club for the past two seasons. It is a great play when it succeeds, but it makes a club look foolish when it fails. Each batter has some simple hit and run sign that all the other men on the club know. The hitter passes this to the base-runner, and the latter should signify by some return signal that he has caught the sign and understands it. A great deal of jockeying helps this play. The batter must hit at the next ball, no matter where it comes, after he gives his sign, because the base-runner is going to start with the pitch, and he will be made to look foolish by the ease with which he is tagged out at second if the batter fails to connect. It is for this reason that the sign for the play should be carefully concealed. If the opposing club is tipped off and expects it, there is no trouble about breaking up the hit and run with a pitch-out, thus catching the base-runner easily at second.

If a man can get on first base and make believe he is going to attempt to steal so the catcher will order a couple of pitch-outs and get the twirler in the hole, the hit and run play will work out more successfully, because then the pitcher has to put the ball over the plate and the batter will have his chance to hit at it. The hit and run play is more appropriate in an open game when a manager desires to take a longer chance. If the club is two or three runs behind, or leading by a safe margin, I would advise it rather than when the game is very close. There is less chance of its going through than the sacrifice, because the batter must first connect with the ball and, second, hit it on the ground, but the returns are bigger when it is successful. If he drives a fly to the infield, the runner has naturally taken such a long start off first base he will be doubled up unless it is a very high pop fly. The batter should try to hit behind the runner, too, the trick I mentioned in the article on batting. The whole purpose of the play is to catch the opposing team off its guard and pick up a flying start for the base-runner, who gets in motion when the pitcher begins his delivery. It takes clever men to work this play and get away with it. The sacrifice is safer when the game is close. But if the batter can make a single on the hit and run, the runner on first will reach third and possibly score. The chances of getting a safe hit are increased because the infield is pulled all out of shape by the premature start of the runner.

Now, if you are behind by a big margin, the club should take more chances. Suppose your opponents have a lead of five runs, one will do you no good. Never sacrifice under these circumstances, but take longer shots for bigger stakes. This is a desperate "stage." Take every chance in the hope that you can rush your opponents off their feet. Once you get them going, often five or six runs may be piled up in an inning before they can stop you. That is the only way to overcome a big lead— by a sudden rally. Instruct your batters to hit it out. Send men home from third if there is the slightest chance of their scoring. Run wild on the bases in the hope that the other team will get throwing around and go up in the air.

There are various "stages" of a game when it is foolish to try to steal a base. Again, the attempt is imperative. If you have a lead of one run or need a run to tie, or if one run is going to make a whole lot of difference to your team and a man reaches first with none out, he should not try to steal. It is too big a risk at that "stage." But suppose, under the same pressing need of one run, a player arrives at first with two out. He cannot score from first base if the batter makes a single, but he probably can from second. Therefore, his object is to reach second as soon as possible. Let him steal at the earliest opportunity when he has any chance at all of success. If he thinks the twirler is playing for him and is going to pitch out on the first ball, it would be ridiculous to try to steal. A man must use his individual judgment under those circumstances. But get down there on second, and you are then in a position to score on a hit. It takes speed and wits to do it.

A great scheme in planning the attack of a ball club is to search for the opposing team's weakness. Most of them have one. If you find that their pitcher is wild, send every man to the bat with orders to take two called strikes before swinging at the ball. This is called "waiting a man out." If it fails to succeed because the pitcher does not lose control, shift suddenly after the twirler has begun to believe he can slip the first two balls over the plate without any danger, he having discovered your waiting tactics, as he would. Tell your men to hit the first ball. Never stick to one system if it is not winning for you.

The infield, with the catcher, plays the most important part in defensive team work. Suppose we consider some specific plays. The destroying of the double steal is a big problem on the defense. It can be worked by outguessing the other side, and it can be broken up by outwitting your opponents. I would not advise selecting any one system for attacking the double steal and sticking to it unwaveringly. Of course, I expect that all my readers know I refer to that delicate situation in a ball game when there is a man on first base and one on third.

If the catcher throws the ball to second, there is grave danger of the runner on third coming home. Yet if no effort is made to get the man going to second, you will lose too many runs in a season to attain any success. You will find that in game after game runs have been scored because that extra man got to second when these tallies would never have been counted if he had been held on first base.

I would recommend to young teams that they try to break up the double steal by the short throw as a regular thing. This requires much accuracy to work it successfully. The shortstop or second baseman runs over behind the pitcher, standing about twenty feet directly in front of second base when he sees the man on first start for second. The catcher drives the ball to him. If the man on third breaks for home, it is up to him to throw back to the catcher, but if he sticks to third, he can turn and toss to the player covering second in time to get the runner coming to second. If this player is smart, he will retrace his tracks toward first so that the ball gets in motion in the resultant effort to run him down, and then the runner on third will dig for home when he sees a good chance.

Other methods of attacking the double steal, which should be employed frequently by way of variety to "cross" the opposing team, are for the catcher to throw directly either to the pitcher or third baseman. If a smart catcher will study closely the styles and weaknesses of base-runners, he can tell the men he will get away from third base on this trick. It is worked as follows:

When the catcher gets the ball, he makes a bluff motion toward second, as if to throw, but does not let go of the ball. The runner on third is on his toes, and seeing this, starts for home. Then the catcher shoots to the third baseman, who tags the runner. You would be surprised at the number of times the man will be caught away from the bag. If the double steal is worked straight, the man on third must start for home as soon as the catcher throws to second to have any chance of success. There are other ways of working the double steal, but this is the most common.

When the ball is thrown to the pitcher, he can shoot it to either second or third. As he whirls, third base comes into his range of vision, and if he sees the runner has started from there, he can deliver the ball to the third baseman. Of course, it is best to get the man nearest home always. If the runner has hugged third base, he can still throw to second with a chance of getting the man going there.

Some leaders recommend drawing their infields in to make the play at the plate whenever a man is on third base and another on first, with less than two out. I prefer trying for the double play unless the game is very close. Of course, if none are out, with men on first and third, you've got to draw the infield in for the play at the plate or sacrifice a run. Or, if there is no one on first, and a man on third, and less than two out, it is again necessary to bring the infield in for the play at the plate. But with men on first and third, with one out, I prefer to try to retire the side on the double play unless the batter is very fast. There is not so much chance with the infield playing back of a ball going through for extra bases. Of course, there arise situations when it is best to make the play at the plate. There are none of these finer situations about which a hard and fast rule can be laid down. The best I can do is suggest the most likely way.

With men on first and second bases and less than two out, I would advise that the first baseman move out of his position about twenty feet down the line, toward the home plate, prepared for a bunt. He should play this bunt to third if he fields it, where the runner is forced. If he sees it is too late to make the play there, he can still toss the ball to first to the second baseman who is covering. The pitcher should make this play in the same way. There is one infallible rule to follow on the defense. Get the man nearest the plate if possible. In this way you save runs. With two out, always make the easiest and surest play.

Infielders must remember to help other infielders. For instance, the third baseman shifts over slightly to cover up the hole left by the shortstop when the latter moves in preparing to cover second base to get a man stealing. Bear in mind you are not nailed fast to one place when playing ball and are expected to move around to meet emergencies.

A complete system of signals should be arranged by the boss of the team, and every man should have these by heart. Do not make the code too complicated. There are the defensive and offensive signs. These include the battery, base running and fielding signs. The leader should be able to signal a base-runner when to steal, and you must have the signal for the hit and run. Every ball club should have a fixed rule about the attitude of the players toward the umpires. They should be treated courteously, protests being made only on a point of the rules.

John McGraw led the New York Giants to ten National League pennants and three World Series championships in 31 years (1902–32) as their manager. *By Charles M. Conlon via Wikimedia Commons.*

CHAPTER 3

A NEW BUSHER BREAKS IN

RING LARDNER

The classic 1914 baseball story, You Know Me Al, by the legendary Ring Lardner, tells the story of the fictional Jack Keefe, a minor league baseball player who earns a trip to the majors to pitch for the Chicago White Sox. It is comprised of letters that Keefe sends to his "old pal" Al. This excerpt captures Keefe's ups and downs during his first few months in the big leagues.

Detroit, Michigan, April 28

FRIEND AL: What do you think of a rotten manager that bawls me out and fines me $50.00 for loosing a 1 to o game in 10 innings when it was my 1st start this season? And no wonder I was a little wild in the 10th when I had not had no chance to work and get control. I got a good notion to quit this rotten club and jump to the Federals where a man gets some kind of treatment. Callahan says I threw the game away on purpose but I did not do no such a thing Al because when I throwed that ball at Joe Hill's head I forgot that the bases was full and besides if Gleason had not of starved me to death the ball that hit him in the head would of killed him.

And how could a man go to 1st base and the winning run be forced in if he was dead which he should ought to of been the lucky left handed stiff if I had of had my full strenth to put on my fast one instead of being 1/2 starved to death and weak. But I guess I better tell you how it come off. The papers will get it all wrong like they generally allways does.

Callahan asked me this A.M. if I thought I was hard enough to work and I was tickled to death because I seen he was going to give me a chance. I told him Sure I was in good shape and if them Tigers scored a run off me he could keep me setting on the bench the rest of the summer. So he says All right I am going to start you and if you go good maybe Gleason will let you eat some supper.

Well Al when I begin warming up I happened to look up in the grand stand and who do you think I seen? Nobody but Violet. She smiled when she seen me but I bet she felt more like crying. Well I smiled back at her because she probily would of broke down and made a seen or something if I had not of. They was not nobody warming up for Detroit when I begin warming up but pretty soon I looked over to their bench and Joe Hill Violet's husband was warming up. I says to myself Well here is where I show that bird up if they got nerve enough to start him against me but probily Jennings don't want to waste no real pitcher on this game which he knows we got cinched and we would of had it cinched Al if they had of got a couple of runs or even 1 run for me.

Well, Jennings come passed our bench just like he allways does and tried to pull some of his funny stuff. He says Hello are you still in the league? I says Yes but I come pretty near not being. I came pretty near being with Detroit. I wish you could of heard Gleason and Callahan laugh when I pulled that one on him. He says something back but it was not no hot comeback like mine.

Well Al if I had of had any work and my regular control I guess I would of pitched a o hit game because the only time they could touch me was when I had to ease up to get them over. Cobb was out of the game and they told me he was sick but I guess the truth is that he knowed I was going to pitch. Crawford got a couple of lucky scratch hits off of me because I got in the hole to him and had to let up. But the way that lucky left handed Hill got by was something awful and if I was as lucky as him I would quit pitching and shoot craps or something.

Our club can't hit nothing anyway. But batting against this bird was just like hitting fungos. His curve ball broke about ½ a inch and you could of wrote your name and address on his fast one while it was comeing up there. He had good control but who would not when they put nothing on the ball?

Well Al we could not get started against the lucky stiff and they could not do nothing with me even if my suport was rotten and I give a couple or 3 or 4 bases on balls but when they was men waiting to score I zipped them threw there so as they could not see them let alone hit them. Every time I come to the bench between innings I looked up to where Violet was setting and give her a smile and she smiled back and once I seen her clapping her hands at me after I had made Moriarty pop up in the pinch.

Well we come along to the 10th inning, o and o, and all of a sudden we got after him. Bodie hits one and Schalk gets 2 strikes and 2 balls and then singles. Callahan tells Alcock to bunt and he does it but Hill sprawls all over himself like the big boob he is and the bases is full with nobody down. Well Gleason and Callahan argude about should they send somebody up for me or let me go up there and I says Let me go up there because I can murder this bird and Callahan says Well they is nobody out so go up and take a wallop.

Honest Al if this guy had of had anything at all I would of hit 1 out of the park, but he did not have even a glove. And how can a man hit pitching which is not no pitching at all but just slopping them up? When I went up there I hollered to him and says Stick 1 over here now you yellow stiff. And he says Yes I can stick them over allright and that is where I got something on you.

Well Al I hit a foul off of him that would of been a fare ball and broke up the game if the wind had not of been against it. Then I swung and missed a curve that I don't see how I missed it. The next 1 was a yard outside and this Evans calls it a strike. He has had it in for me ever since last year when he tried to get funny with me and I says something back to him that stung him. So he calls this 3d strike on me and I felt like murdering him. But what is the use?

I throwed down my bat and come back to the bench and I was glad Callahan and Gleason was out on the coaching line or they pro-bily would of said something to me and I would of cut loose and beat them up. Well Al Weaver and Blackburne looked like a couple of rums up there and we don't score where we ought to of had 3 or 4 runs with any kind of hitting.

I would of been all O. K. in spite of that peace of rotten luck if this big Hill had of walked to the bench and not said nothing like a real pitcher. But what does he do but wait out there till I start for the box and I says Get on to the bench you lucky stiff or do you want me to hand you something? He says I don't want nothing more of yourn. I allready got your girl and your goat.

Well Al what do you think of a man that would say a thing like that? And nobody but a left hander could of. If I had of had a gun I would of killed him deader than a doornail or something. He starts for the bench and I hollered at him Wait till you get up to that plate an then I am going to bean you. Honest Al I was so mad I could not see the plate or nothing. I don't even know who it was come up to bat ist but whoever it was I hit him in the arm and he walks to first base. The next guy bunts and Chase tries to pull off i of them plays of hisn instead of playing safe and he don't get nobody. Well 1 kept getting madder and madder and I walks Stanage who if I had of been myself would not foul me.

Callahan has Scotty warming up and Gleason runs out from the bench and tells me I am threw but Callahan says Wait a minute he is going to let Hill hit and this big stiff ought to be able to get him out of the way and that will give Scotty a chance to get warm. Gleason says You better not take a chance because the big busher is hogwild, and they kept argueing till I got sick of listening to them and I went back to the box and got ready to pitch. But when I seen this Hill up there I forgot all about the ball game and I cut loose at his bean.

Well Al my control was all O. K. this time and I catched him square on the fourhead and he dropped like as if he had been shot. But pretty soon he gets up and gives me the laugh and runs to first base. I did not know the game was over till Weaver come up and pulled me off the field. But if I had not of been 1/2 starved to death and weak so as I could not put all my stuff on the ball you can bet that Hill never would of ran to first base and Violet would of been a widow and probily a lot better off than she is now. At that I never should ought to of tried to kill a left-hander by hitting him in the head.

Well Al they jumped all over me in the clubhouse and I had to hold myself back or I would of gave somebody the beating of their life.

Callahan tells me I am fined $50.00 and suspended without no pay, I asked him What for and he says They would not be no use in telling you because you have not got no brains. I says Yes I have to got some brains and he says Yes but they is in your stumach. And then he says I wish we had of* sent you to Milwaukee and I come back at him. I says I wish you had of.

Well Al I guess they is no chance of getting square treatment on this club and you won't be supprised if you hear of me jumping to the Federals where a man is treated like a man and not like no white slave.

Yours truly, JACK.

Chicago, Illinois, May 2

AL: I have got to disappoint you again Al. When I got up to get my pay yesterday they held out $150.00 on me. $50.00 of it is what I was fined for loosing a 1 to 0 10-inning game in Detroit when I was so weak that I should ought never to of been sent in there and the $100.00 is the advance money that I drawed last winter and which I had forgot all about and the club would of forgot about it to if they was not so tight fisted.

So you see all I get for 2 weeks' pay is about $80.00 and I sent $25.00 to Florrie so she can't come no none support business on me.

I am still suspended Al and not drawing no pay now and I got a notion to hire a attorney at law and force them to pay my salery or else jump to the Federals where a man gets good treatment.

Allen is still after me to come over to his flat some night and see his wife and let her talk to me about Florrie but what do I want to talk about Florrie for or talk about nothing to a nut left hander's wife?

Chicago White Sox manager Jimmy (Nixey) Callahan. *By Bain News Service via Wikimedia Commons.*

The Detroit Club is here and Cobb is playing because he knows I am suspended but I wish Callahan would call it off and let me work against them and I would certainly love to work against this Joe Hill again and I bet they would be a different story this time because I been getting something to eat since we been home and I got back most of my strenth.

Your old pal, JACK.

Chicago, Illinois, May 5

FRIEND AL: Well Al if you been reading the papers you will know before this letter is received what I done. Before the Detroit Club come here Joe Hill had win 4 strate but he has not win no 5 strate or won't neither Al because I put a crimp in his winning streek just like I knowed I would do if I got a chance when I was feeling good and had all my strenth. Callahan asked me yesterday A.M. if 1 thought I had enough rest and I says Sure because I did not need no rest in the ist place. Well, he says, I thought maybe if I layed you off a few days you would do some thinking and if you done some thinking once in a while you would be a better pitcher.

Well anyway I worked and I wish you could of saw them Tigers trying to hit me Cobb and Crawford incluseive. The ist time Cobb come up Weaver catched a lucky line drive off of him and the next time I eased up a little and Collins run back and took a fly ball off of the fence. But the other times he come up he looked like a sucker except when he come up in the 8th and then he beat out a bunt but allmost anybody is liable to do that once in a while.

Crawford got a scratch hit between Chase and Blackburne in the 2d inning and in the 4th he was gave a three-base hit by this Evans who should ought to be writeing for the papers instead of trying to umpire. The ball was 2 feet foul and I bet Crawford will tell you the same thing if you ask him. But what I done to this Hill was awful. I give him my curve twice when he was up there in the 3d and he missed it a foot. Then I come with my fast ball right past his nose and I bet if he had not of ducked it would of drove that big horn of hisn clear up in the press box where them rotten reporters sits and smokes their hops. Then when he was looking for another fast one I slopped up my slow one and he is still swinging at it yet.

But the best of it was that I practally won my own game. Bodie and Schalk was on when I come up in the 5th and Hill hollers to me and says I guess this is where I shoot one of them bean balls. I says Go ahead and shoot and if you hit me in the head and I ever find it out I will write and tell your wife what happened to you. You see what I was getting at Al. I was insinuating that if he beaned me with his fast one I would not never know nothing about it if somebody did not tell me because his fast one is not fast enough to hurt nobody even if it should hit them in the head. So I says to him Go ahead and shoot and if you hit me in the head and I ever find it out I will write and tell your wife what happened to you. See, Al?

Of coarse you could not hire me to write to Violet but I did not mean that part of it in ernest. Well sure enough he shot at my bean and I ducked out of the way though if it had of hit me it could not of did no more than tickle. He takes 2 more shots and misses me and then Jennings hollers from the bench What are you doing pitching or trying to win a cigar? So then Hill sees what a monkey he is makeing out of himself and tries to get one over, but I have him 3 balls and nothing and what I done to that groover was a plenty. She went over Bush's head like a bullet and got between Cobb and Veach and goes clear to

South Side " White Sox " Ball Park, Chicago.

Comiskey Park, home of the Chicago White Sox, opened in 1909. *By Franklin Post Card Co. via Wikimedia Commons*

the fence. Bodie and Schalk scores and I would of scored to if anybody else beside Cobb had of been chaseing the ball. I got 2 bases and Weaver scores me with another wallop.

Say, I wish I could of heard what they said to that baby on the bench. Callahan was tickled to death and he says Maybe I will give you back that $50.00 if you keep that stuff up. I guess I will get that $50.00 back next pay day and if I do Al I will pay you the hole $75.00.

Well Al I beat them 5 to 4 and with good support I would of held them to 1 run but what do I care as long as I beat them? I wish though that Violet could of been there and saw it.

Yours truly, JACK.

Chicago, Illinois, May 29

OLD PAL: Well Al I have not wrote to you for a long while but it is not because I have forgot you and to show I have not forgot you I am incloseing the $75.00 which I owe you. It is a money order Al and you can get it cashed by takeing it to Joe Higgins at the P. O.

Since I wrote to you Al I been East with the club and I guess you know what I done in the East. The Athaletics did not have no right to win that 1 game off of me and I will get them when they come here the week after next. I beat Boston and just as good as beat New York twice because I beat them 1 game all alone and then saved the other for Eddie Cicotte in the 9th inning and shut out the Washington Club and would of did the same thing if Johnson had of been working against me instead of this left handed stiff Boehling.

Speaking of left handers Allen has been going rotten and I would not be supprised if they sent him to Milwaukee or Frisco or somewheres.

But I got bigger news than that for you Al. Florrie is back and we are liveing together in the spair room at Allen's flat so I hope they don't send him to Milwaukee or nowheres else because it is not costing us nothing for room rent and this is no more than right after the way the Allens grafted off of us all last winter.

I bet you will be supprised to know that I and Florrie has made it up and they is a secret about it Al which I can't tell you now but maybe next month I will tell you and then you will be more supprised than ever. It is about I and Florrie and somebody else. But that is all I can tell you now.

We got in this A.M. Al and when I got to my room they was a slip of paper there telling me to call up a phone number so I called it up and it was Allen's flat and Marie answered the phone. And when

I reckonized her voice I was going to hang up the phone but she says Wait a minute somebody wants to talk to you. And then Florrie come to the phone and I was going to hang up the phone again when she pulled this secret on me that I was telling you about.

So it is all fixed up between us Al and I wish I could tell you the secret but that will come later. I have tooken my baggage over to Allen's and I am there now writeing to you while Florrie is asleep. And after a while I am going out and mail this letter and get a glass of beer because I think I have got 1 comeing now on account of this secret. Florrie says she is sorry for the way she treated me and she cried when she seen me. So what is the use of me being nasty Al? And let bygones be bygones.

Your pal, JACK.

Chicago, Illinois, June 26

FRIEND AL: Al I beat the Athaletics 2 to 1 to-day but I am writeing to you to give you the supprise of your life. Old pal I got a baby and he is a boy and we are going to name him Allen which Florrie thinks is after his uncle and aunt Allen but which is after you old pal. And she can call him Allen but I will call him Al because I don't never go back on my old pals. The baby was born over to the hospital and it is going to cost me a bunch of money but I should not worry. This is the secret I was going to tell you Al and I am the happyest man in the world and I bet you are most as tickled to death to hear about it as I am.

The baby was born just about the time I was makeing McInnis look like a sucker in the pinch but they did not tell me nothing about it till after the game and then they give me a phone messige in the clubhouse. I went right over there and everything was all O. K. Little Al is a homely little skate but I guess all babys is homely and don't have no looks till they get older and maybe he will look like Florrie or I then I won't have no kick comeing.

Be sure and tell Bertha the good news and tell her everything has came out all right except that the rent man is still after me about that flat I had last winter. And I am still paying the old man $10.00 a month for that house you got for me and which has not never done me no good. But I should not worry about money when I got a real family. Do you get that Al, a real family?

Well Al I am to happy to do no more writeing tonight but I wanted you to be the 1st to get the news and I would of sent you a telegram only I did not want to scare you.

Your pal, JACK.

Chicago, Illinois, July 2

OLD PAL: Well old pal I just come back from St. Louis this A.M. and found things in pretty fare shape. Florrie and the baby is out to Allen's and we will stay there till I can find another place. The Dr. was out to look at the baby this A.M. and the baby was waveing his arm round in the air. And Florrie asked was they something the matter with him that he kept waveing his arm. And the Dr. says No he was just getting his exercise.

Well Al I noticed that he never waved his right arm but kept waveing his left arm and I asked the Dr. why was that. Then the Dr. says I guess he must be left handed. That made me sore and I says I guess you doctors don't know it all. And then I turned round and beat it out of the room.

Well Al it would be just my luck to have him left handed and Florrie should ought to of knew better than to name him after Allen. I am going to hire another Dr. and see what he has to say because they must be some way of fixing babys so as they won't be left handed. And if necessary I will cut his left arm off of him. Of coarse I would not do that Al. But how would I feel if a boy of mine turned out like Allen and Joe Hill and some of them other nuts?

We have a game with St. Louis tomorrow and a double header on the 4th of July. I guess probily Callahan will work me in one of the 4th of July games on account of the holiday crowd.

Your pal, JACK.

P. S. Maybe I should ought to leave the kid left handed so as he can have some of their luck. The lucky stiffs.

CHAPTER 4

RIDING THE RAILS

JACK CAVANAUGH

If hardly any American civilians were traveling by ship in 1942, more Americans than ever were traveling by train, including hundreds of thousands of servicemen. So, too, were big league baseball teams, which were still doing so until the 1950s. As the western-most teams, the St. Louis Cardinals and the St. Louis Browns logged the most miles, sometimes spending up to twenty-four hours or more on trips from St. Louis to Boston. "It resulted in a far greater camaraderie than you have on ball clubs today, because you spent so much time together," said Don Gutteridge, who spent five years with the Cardinals during the Gas House era and then four years with the Browns during a twelve-year career that ended with brief stays with the Red Sox and the Pirates and a two-year stint as manager of the White Sox. "We ate together in the dining car, played cards together, slept together in the Pullman cars, and talked baseball by the hour." Enos Slaughter, a teammate of Gutteridge when both played for the Cardinals in the late 1930s, agreed: "They talk about family on some clubs nowadays, but when you traveled by train, you really were a family." Slaughter rode trains during eighteen of the nineteen years of his Hall of Fame career. "Now players drive to an airport, get on the team plane, maybe go to sleep, fly to wherever they're playing next, and go to their hotel room, and then to the ballpark the next day.

Hall of Famer Enos Slaughter, shown here as a New York Yankee in 1957, rode trains for eighteen of his nineteen years in the majors. *AP Photo*.

Now, especially at home, a lot of players only get to see each other at the ballpark."

Former Red Sox second baseman Bobby Doerr said he much preferred traveling by train than flying. "Near the end of my career, we had a choice of flying or going by train, and I'd always go by train," Doerr said. "It was much more relaxing than flying, and it brought the players closer together. When we were traveling between Chicago and St. Louis, I loved just sitting and looking out the window at farmland. It was both enjoyable and relaxing."

Most baseball teams chartered three private cars—two sleeping cars and a dining car, which also served as a lounge—that could be coupled to a regular train. In 1942 and the subsequent three years of the war, though, teams shared diners and club cars with sometimes awestruck riders, who couldn't believe they were eating in the same car as Ted Williams or Joe DiMaggio. For the most part, the players kept to themselves, but there were exceptions. "If Pepper Martin heard there was, say, a group of Shriners or Boy Scouts on the train, he'd go down and talk to them, play his harmonica, and sign autographs," said catcher Mickey Owen, who spent several seasons playing with Martin on the Cardinals in the late 1930s. "Sometimes, he'd bring the Mudcats along. The Mudcats also would break out their instruments and practice for hours on train trips, and sometimes they'd go marching through the train, playing and attracting crowds. It was really something to see." And no doubt to hear.

Though the Gas House Gang had a reputation for being a rollicking collection of characters, it had its share of internal strife. Owen recalled how, during a game of poker aboard a train, Paul "Daffy" Dean, the younger brother of Dizzy Dean, with whom he played for the Cardinals from 1934 through 1937, implied that Joe Medwick had not anted up.

"Joe was furious and said to Paul, 'Are you calling me a thief?'" Without waiting for an answer, Owen said, Medwick, always ready for a fight, punched Dean in the nose. "Blood spurted from Paul's nose, and I think Joe felt he had killed him," Owen said. "But Paul never flinched, and Joe backed off, realizing that Paul had taken his best shot without going down. Paul then jumped on Joe and began to bang away before some of the guys pulled him off. It was totally out of character for Paul, who was a quiet, easygoing guy, not at all like Dizzy, and never got into fights."

Getting into fights was not out of character for Pete Gray, the one-armed outfielder, who spent the 1945 season with the Browns. "Pete was a helluva ballplayer but had a chip on his shoulder a mile wide," said infielder Ellis Clary, who was a teammate of Gray in 1945. Clary recalled a near fight involving Gray on a railroad station platform in Toledo. "We were waiting for a train after playing an exhibition game against our Toledo farm club," Clary said. "There was a barrel of fish on the platform, and someone took one of the fish out of the barrel, then sneaked up behind Pete, and put the fish in his left pocket, where he kept his cigarettes. When Pete reached in the pocket for his cigarettes and found the fish, he went right at Sig Jakucki, a big pitcher who outweighed Pete by about fifty pounds and was always pulling pranks on him. Pete suspected that Jakucki had done it and hauled off and punched him in the chest. If some of the guys hadn't grabbed Sig, he might have killed Pete on that platform." Despite such incidents and Gray's tendency to rebuff any efforts to make things easier for him in general, he appeared in seventy-seven games and got fifty-one hits in 234 times at bat while striking out only eleven times and batting .218, a higher average than that of many big league outfielders with two arms who three and four decades later were earning more than $1 million and not necessarily performing as well in the outfield.

An even more memorable fight than the one between Gray and Jakucki occurred on a train carrying the Yankees from Kansas City to Detroit after they had clinched the American League pennant in 1958. The Bronx Bombers were celebrating the occasion with champagne that night when Ralph Houk, then a coach with the Yankees, prepared to light up a victory cigar. As he did, relief pitcher Ryne Duren sneaked up behind him and playfully, or at least playfully to Duren, squashed the cigar in Houk's face. According to some accounts, Houk, who was renowned for his quick temper, responded by decking Duren with a punch. Other witnesses said Houk, who had served at the Battle of the Bulge and was known as the Iron Major—having been a major in the army—floored Duren with the back of his hand.

For younger players, the train carrying a team could sometimes be a classroom of sorts. "A lot of the veterans would take young players aside on the train and tell them what to expect from other teams they were going to face," Don Gutteridge said. "At the beginning of my career, I learned an awful lot from some of the older guys while riding the trains."

Owen's recollections were similar. "I recall sitting on the train with pitchers like Lon Warneke and Curt Davis, who would tell me about different hitters," said Owen, an outstanding catcher, although best remembered for letting a pitch from Hugh Casey get away from him that cost the Dodgers a win in the 1941 World Series. "Sometimes, especially during the war, you'd find yourself on trains with other teams. I remember how, once, when I was a young catcher with the Cardinals, Jimmy Wilson, a great catcher who was managing the Phillies at the time, spent an hour with me in the washroom showing me the best way to put a tag on a runner. He was the best tagger I ever saw, and he helped me tremendously."

But in addition to the long hours, train travel had some other drawbacks. "When I came up [in 1935], the trains were not air-conditioned," said Terry Moore, who played for the Cardinals from 1935 through 1948. (He did not play from 1943–45 due to his being in the military.) "We'd spent a lot of time in the diners, which were cooled by ice. But on hot nights, we'd open the windows to get some air and then wake up covered with soot and cinders from the locomotives."

Mel Allen, who broadcast Yankee games in the 1940s and 1950s, said, "The train was a rollicking clubhouse. Casey Stengel would roam through the cars, delighting passengers with his stories or making speeches in the dining car that just about everyone on the entire train could hear. And everyone, the players, coaches, managers, writers, and broadcasters, spent a lot of time together on the train trips."

Jack Lang, who covered the Dodgers and later the New York Mets for the defunct *Long Island Press* and later for the *New York Daily News*, said his job was both easier and more difficult in the train-traveling days. "The players were far more accessible on the trains," Lang told me years ago. "In a way, they were a captive audience, and the writers got to know them much better." But when it came to filing stories, things were less rosy for the beat writers. "Quite often you'd have to hurry to catch the train after a game, so you'd have to write your story on the train. Fortunately, if you were writing for a morning paper, you still had time, since most games were played in the afternoon," Lang recalled. "If you left Cincinnati, for example, you'd have an hour and a half to get your story done before the train reached Indianapolis, where a Western Union operator would be waiting. So you had to have the story done by then, because there was no other way to file your story."

Planes, of course, occasionally encounter turbulence, but then trains also could have their rough moments, as Hall of Fame shortstop and later manager Lou Boudreau recollected. "The train would go around a bad curve, and it would wake you up," Boudreau said. "Or you'd be awakened while the train was going along a bad stretch of track."

Like Pepper Martin and Casey Stengel, Babe Ruth also liked to roam through a train. "Babe loved people, and he'd wander through the train, talking to passengers, who loved meeting him," said Jimmie Reese, who roomed with Ruth in 1930 and 1931 when he was a utility infielder for the Yankees. "I'll never forget the time Jake Ruppert [then the owner of the Yankees] was aboard the train, and Babe picked him up and threw him into an upper berth," Reese, a longtime coach for the then-California Angels, said. "No one else would have ever dared to do a thing like that." By the 1950s, most players had their own roomettes aboard the team trains. But in the earlier years, players slept in upper and lower berths in Pullman cars. "The veterans got the lower berths, and the younger players the uppers," said Reese, who was still hitting fungoes for the Angels while in his mid-eighties. "But when I was with the Yankees, Babe had his own drawing room on the train, something that, as a rule, only managers and coaches had."

Ruth was the central figure in one of the legendary episodes of baseball train travel. "The Yankees were about to leave Shreveport, Louisiana, during a spring training trip in 1925, when, suddenly, the Babe came running through the train, followed by a woman with a knife," recalled Red Foley, a former baseball writer for the *New York Daily News*. "When he got to the observation car at the end of the train, he jumped off and onto the platform to escape the woman, who was still right behind him. She finally got off, too, and then Babe managed to jump on the train as it started leaving the station."

Dave Anderson, then a young sportswriter for the old *Brooklyn Eagle*, also found himself pursued on a train, albeit in a less dangerous fashion, by no less than one of his all-time favorite athletes, Jackie Robinson. "I was talking to Roy Campanella [the Brooklyn Dodgers Hall of Fame catcher] in the Dodgers' clubhouse after a close game that the Dodgers had lost to the Giants," Anderson recalled:

Jackie was still furious about an umpire's call and that shrill voice of his became louder and louder. Finally, Campanella said, and he said it quietly, "Oh, Robinson, why don't you shut up," and I used the quote in my story the following day. That night we were leaving by train on a road trip when somebody told me on the railroad platform at Penn Station that Robinson was looking for me. I asked why, and he told me it was because of the Campanella quote. I had thought the quote was funny, since I don't think Campy was really serious when he said it. But I was told that Jackie didn't see it that way. A short while later while I was in my roomette in one of the three cars the Dodgers usually had on a train, I heard Jackie's voice loud and clear from one of the other cars, and then nearer and nearer, saying, "Where's that Dave Anderson? I'm going to kick his ass." He finally got to my roomette, where I was sitting down with the door open, since I knew there was no point in trying to hide. Jackie, obviously very mad, stared down at me, and said, "You made me look bad in front of my teammates by using that quote, and I'm going to kick your ass." I told Jackie to take it easy and that Campanella was smiling when he said it, and readers probably understood that he wasn't being serious. But Jack said he didn't think so, and I kept saying I thought they would, after which he finally left. He never mentioned the quote again, and we had a good relationship from then on.

Anderson said he treasured the memory of the incident, because, as he said in his book *Sports of Our Times,* "For once I had seen Jackie Robinson the way his opponents often had—in full flame out."

For Don Gutteridge, who never had to worry about being pursued on a train by Jackie Robinson, traveling by train was a joyful experience, especially at night. "I still remember the clickety-clack sound of the train on the tracks," Gutteridge said years ago. "It was the most marvelous sound to go to sleep by, and I never slept better than on the train. It took a lot longer than it does by plane, but I loved traveling across the country by train. Someday I'm going to get back on the train and take some of the same long trips that we did many years ago. I bet I'll sleep better than ever."

CHAPTER 5

THE BLACK SOX CONSPIRACY UNFOLDS

TIM HORNBAKER

Most of what is currently understood about the 1919 scandal nearly a hundred years after the fact is still open to debate and interpretation. There are many different versions of what happened and it is nearly impossible to say with absolute certainty that "this or that account is exactly what occurred" between the members of the White Sox and their gambling counterparts. For instance, a number of newspaper outlets would later claim that Hal Chase, the infamous first baseman, was the linchpin for the entire conspiracy. The allegations surfaced that Chase was responsible for bringing both Abe Attell and Bill Burns onboard, and that it was Attell, not Gandil, who initially reached out to Sullivan with an assist from Chase.[1] Yet another depiction claimed that Sullivan was the point of origin for the fix, and that he went to Gandil with the idea.[2] But there are clear and obvious discrepancies, and enough doubt is cast to offer the necessary reminder that the story of the 1919 scandal is anything but cut and dry.

With regard to Joe Jackson, there is an important question: did he have any other legitimate reasons to consider endangering his baseball future in such a shaky proposition other than being coerced by the statement that the fix was on whether he was involved or not? The simple answer is yes, he did. With the goal of attaining $20,000 for his participation, Jackson anticipated raking in more than three years' salary in one series. Joe had previously admitted that he was fully content with leaving baseball behind after obtaining enough money, and that he was eager to settle into a quieter farm life.[3] But that was in 1912, and Jackson was a much different man in 1919 than he was at that time. He was still interested in making money, but his baseball success had made him one of the most popular stars in the game. Leaving the sport on short notice made little sense, especially since his career was progressing so well and he was likely headed toward immortal glory with his peers in any future hall of fame.

But Jackson was much more sensitive. For a period of seven to eight months between May 1918 and January 1919, he was relentlessly abused and shamed by the press corps. Baseball writers, editorials, and other commentaries slammed his decision to work in the shipyards, condemning him in nearly every way possible. The constant remarks were humiliating, drawing into question his manhood, his ethical sensibilities, his devotion to his country, and every word took its toll. He even told a reporter during the midst of all the chaos, "I shall not attempt to go back to ball playing to make a living."[4] Jackson was undoubtedly saddened by the overwhelming backlash and knew that some of the reporter's resentment had trickled down to the public, as well. It was completely unwarranted, he felt, and he managed to live with the criticism each day. Only nine months had passed since the bulk of the condemnation ceased, and not all had been forgotten.

In fact, some fans wouldn't let him forget. During a trip to Detroit in early September 1919, rowdy spectators yelled "shipyards!" at Jackson, hoping to interfere with his game-time concentration.[5] He was usually able to ignore the drunken outbursts of instigators, but the symbolism behind such remarks did nothing but remind everyone of the cruelty he'd received. Within the White Sox camp itself, there were issues that remained unresolved, and much of it related to owner Charles Comiskey. In February, sportswriter George S. Robbins boldly declared: "Jackson has been manhandled and lambasted in a rough manner here, and President Comiskey himself is responsible for the feeling to a great degree, for Commy never has retracted in print what he said about Joe."[6] In another column, Robbins wrote: "We would like to see Commy come out in the open and give Jackson the glad hand. If Comiskey is lukewarm about Jackson, he can't expect the fans to be any other way, especially those who panned him last summer."[7]

While it is not known what, if anything, was said between Comiskey and Jackson in private, it is not believed "The Old Roman" made a public statement withdrawing his previous criticisms. That in itself was enough to leave Joe with a bad taste in his mouth about the Sox, and taking all things into consideration leaves the question: how much real passion did he still have for baseball? He played solid ball in 1919, and his natural abilities were evident as much at the plate as they were in the field. But what was his mind-set? Is it possible that he had anything but animosity toward Comiskey and the press for what he'd been put through? Did he want revenge? Or did he see the $20,000 he was to receive in the fix as a way to finally break free from the Sox and baseball forever?

His agreement to be a part of the conspiracy, and the peace he made with his own conscience as to what was about to happen, might have been predicated, in part, on that fact. But Jackson wasn't a natural schemer, nor was he a gambler. The details of the scam were far outside his realm of understanding. He didn't comprehend the bigger picture: where the growing nature of the fix involved dozens and dozens of components. Jackson didn't understand that such a revelation jeopardized his good name inside and outside of baseball and made him susceptible to any number of potential dangers, including criminal prosecution. Everything he'd worked for throughout his life—his upstanding reputation, his idol status among kids, his astronomical lifetime batting average—would forever be tainted in such an instance, and Joe was either too unaware to understand or just felt the reward outweighed the risk.

A number of secret meetings about the soon-to-be-rigged Series were staged before the White Sox officially captured the American League pennant on September 24, 1919. Jackson contributed two hits in the 6–5 triumph over the St. Louis Browns, and the home crowd at Comiskey Park was thoroughly enthused by the victory.[8] However, many of those same fans were equally disappointed by the performance of the Sox in their subsequent four games, which were the final contests of the regular season. Instead of finishing the campaign with a commanding display of their abilities, Chicago lost all four (one to St. Louis and three against Detroit). "I was extremely sorry to see the Sox play the manner of ball they revealed yesterday," explained longtime fan Dad Kentmor. "It pained me deeply to see our boys play that way. It has been said they are the greatest money team ever assembled, and I guess that is the right dope. There was nothing at stake for them yesterday and they played like a bunch of amateurs."[9]

It was another "money team" reference, but this time made by a fan. Kentmor went on to say, "In the World's Series they will play wonderful ball because they have the incentive of the winning end of the melon before them." Harvey T. Woodruff of the *Chicago Daily Tribune* seemed to agree, pegging the Sox to win over their National League opponents, the Cincinnati Reds. He actually referred to Kid Gleason's club as the "greatest aggregation of money players in baseball."[10] The same went for George S. Robbins, who made a striking comment in the August 28, 1919, edition of the *Sporting News* in sizing up Comiskey's players going into the series: "The Sox are great money players. Show that gang a bunch of coin and they'll do almost anything except commit murder."[11] No one outside the secretive cabal grinding away on the Series fix knew just how accurate the words "money team" were, as the corrupt members of the Sox plotted a record monetary output for players in the event's history. They were forging ahead without the consent of owners to their financial score and weren't exactly getting executive approval from the National Baseball Commission.

Chick Gandil, Swede Risberg, and Fred McMullin were motivated to go ahead with the idea from its inception. With Gandil leading the way, the trio planned a special confab for the Warner Hotel in Chicago—not overly far from Comiskey Park on the South Side—on September 29, 1919. According to the later recollections of Lefty Williams, who attended the meeting, the roster of participants included Gandil, Eddie Cicotte, Happy Felsch, Buck Weaver, plus the Boston gambler "Sport" Sullivan and his ally "Brown," who was later identified as Rachael Brown.[12] Joe Jackson wasn't present, but, by the end of the meeting, a total of eight Sox players were officially tied to the fix whether they wanted to be or not. There was no way to disavow knowledge of what was going to be attempted, and if anyone wanted to back out, the only way was to spill the beans to an outsider and throw his teammates at the mercy of the law.

For the conspirators, having Jackson involved was a major coup. His hard hitting was certainly a key to Chicago's success, and his participation inspired confidence in their ability to follow through. But Eddie Cicotte was even more important. The right-handed pitching ace was going to start two, possibly three games during the Series, and if he was lobbing them over the plate, how could the scheme fail? Cicotte, known for his intelligence, took his time in deciding whether or not to play ball with Gandil and thoroughly weighed his options. Money, he decided, was the answer to his problems, particularly when it came to paying off his farm's sizable mortgage, and so agreed.[13]

The winner of 29 games during the regular season, Cicotte was acknowledged as one of the sport's finest pitchers, and he told a reporter earlier in 1919 that he could easily pitch for another ten years.[14] But with just half that time as a pro, his status as a future Hall of Famer was pretty much guaranteed. So, like Jackson, he had plenty to lose. Unlike Jackson, Cicotte smartly demanded $10,000 in cash up front and refused to commit his services unless the money was in his possession prior to the start of Game One. "I didn't want any promises," he later admitted.[15] But promises were precisely what Jackson was banking on, taking Gandil at his word that increments of cash would be delivered promptly after each game.[16]

With the World Series fast approaching, sportswriters offered detailed analysis of the two clubs, comparing and contrasting their various styles. The Cincinnati Reds were a balanced group led by manager Pat Moran and finished their pennant race with a nine-game advantage over the second-place New York Giants. Center fielder Edd Roush, who began his career with the Sox as a twenty-year-old in 1913, was not only leading the Reds in hitting but the entire National League with a .321 average. Third baseman Heinie Groh was fourth in the league with a .310 average, while three other starters were in the .270 range. As a club, Cincinnati was hitting .263, tied for second in the league with the Brooklyn Robins, and six points behind the Giants. Pitching was the Reds' strength, and Moran had five reliable starters: two lefties and three right-handers. Southpaw Slim Sallee was on the losing end of the 1917 Series as a member of the Giants and was looking for a bit of revenge. His 21 regular season wins were second in the league.[17]

Conversely, the Sox still lacked depth on the mound, but Kid Gleason wasn't worried. He believed in his top two pitchers, knowing that Eddie Cicotte and Lefty Williams had enough talent, conditioning, and resiliency to overcome whatever challenges they faced against the Reds. He also gave them time to recover from the strain of the regular season. "Cicotte says his arm hasn't a trace of lameness," Gleason told a reporter on September 30, "and that means Eddie is ready for the World's Series of 1919. About the only worry I had was Eddie and now I have none."[18] Harry Neily of the *Chicago American* once wrote that Gleason knew "more about the White Sox than anybody in the world," and if he was confident in the shape of his men headed into the Series, who was to doubt him?[19] But Gleason had no clue that Cicotte and Williams were now on the take, and with his star hurlers intentionally trying to lose, the Sox were doomed before the first Series pitch was thrown.

On the political side of things, a majority of owners voted in favor of extending the Series from seven to nine games. The move was sponsored by National Commission chairman Garry Herrmann, and Sox supporters figured it was a sly way for Herrmann to assist Cincinnati because of Chicago's limited pitching staff. After all, Herrmann was also a part owner of the Reds. Charles Comiskey was the only man in both leagues to vote against the change, even though the maneuver guaranteed more money for him in the long run. However, he denied his vote had anything to do with his club's limitations.[20] Comiskey wasn't stupid, though, and was keenly aware of how things stood. At that same time, he was holding a personal grudge against his former friend, American League President Ban Johnson, as to the way the latter and the National Commission handled the rights to veteran right-hander Jack Quinn, who was sent to the New York Yankees after Quinn had pitched for the Sox in 1918. Quinn would've potentially filled Chicago's need as a third or fourth starter, and Comiskey was still sore.

The tainted members of the White Sox received their marching orders, the gamblers placed their bets, and the home plate umpire called for "play ball" on Wednesday, October 1, 1919. Over 30,000 people watched from the stands at Redland Field for Game One in

The 1919 Chicago White Sox original news photograph. *By International Film Service via Wikimedia Commons.*

Cincinnati, as Cicotte took the mound in the bottom of the first inning. Facing second baseman Morrie Rath—another former Sox cast-off—Cicotte threw the first pitch for a called strike. The next sailed high and hit Rath directly in his shoulder, giving him first base.[21] Only later was it revealed that Cicotte's errant pitch wasn't an accident, but purposeful. By hitting Rath, he silently conveyed the message that the fix was on.

Due to the nature of his state of mind in 1919, his afternoon on the mound was no better against the Reds. He pitched for 3 2/3 innings, giving up six runs on seven hits with two walks before Gleason had enough and pulled him. Jackson made his first plate appearance in the second inning, leading off against Dutch Ruether, and slashed one at shortstop Larry Kopf. The latter bobbled the ball and then proceeded to throw it over the first baseman's head, allowing Jackson to reach second on the error. Happy Felsch sacrificed him to third and Chick Gandil singled him home for the first Chicago run . . . their only score of the contest.[22]

The rest of the game was relatively uneventful for the White Sox, with Jackson going 0-for-4 at the plate. The Reds, on the other hand, pummeled Sox pitching for nine runs and 14 hits, winning 9–1. Shano Collins, who started in right field for the Sox, later admitted that by the first game, rumors of a fix had circulated throughout the clubhouse. "I had heard some talk but we all laughed at it," he explained. "Cicotte of course had been badly beaten in the opening game. But we were willing to make allowances for that. You see 'Knuckles' had been complaining of a sore arm during the last month of the regular season. [Additionally], we were willing to accept the explanation that he gave . . . that McMullin had scouted the Reds for two weeks and that he, Cicotte, had pitched according to McMullin's dope, all of which he said was wrong. So we figured it was only an off day for him."[23]

But Collins was in the dark to the genuine truth that his teammates were indeed crooked. In fact, behind the closed doors of the club's hotel, Jackson inquired to Gandil about the first installment of his owed money.[24] Gandil didn't have a good answer. He reportedly was given the shaft by Bill Burns and Abe Attell, leaving the players high and dry.[25] More promises were made, and players were again ordered to lose in Game Two the following day. Lefty Williams went to the mound and held the Reds to only four hits, but gave up four costly earned runs. "Our second defeat . . . when Lefty Williams was on the rubber, was unexpected," Collins told a reporter. "In this game we outhit the Reds better than two to one and yet we were hopelessly beaten. Of course, Williams's wildness was mainly responsible. But long afterwards in comparing the respective scores and figuring our ten hits against the Reds four we made note of the fact that none of our ten hits came at the right time."[26]

Jackson achieved his first hit of the Series in the second inning when he smashed a double to left-center but was stranded at third when the inning closed. In the fourth, he followed Buck Weaver's single with one of his own, but subsequent batters failed to move them along. Joe had an opportunity in the sixth to drive home a run with Weaver on second but struck out on three straight pitches. He achieved his third hit of the afternoon in the eighth with two outs, but it had no influence on the game's final totals.[27] And with that the Reds were victorious in Game Two, 4–2. With the Series heading to Chicago for Game Three, players checked out of their hotel and boarded a train westward. While en route, they discussed the two previous games at length, trying to get a beat on what was happening, but were incredibly stumped by the turn of events.[28]

Once again, Jackson asked Gandil about his money, and again Chick didn't have a response other than to blame Burns and Attell for not fulfilling their part of the deal.[29] The crooked players had done their part, purposefully striving to lose the first two games of the Series.

Looking at Jackson's performance, the question to be asked was: what had he contributed to the fix? He'd gone 3-for-8 at the plate for a .375 batting average, garnered a double and a run, and played flawlessly in the field. Twice he went to bat with men in scoring position—in the sixth inning of both the first and second games—but failed to produce. In the past, when Jackson was having a bad day or acting indifferently on the field, everyone knew it. For instance, a writer for the *Cleveland Leader* in 1912 noted seeing Joe "loaf" going after a ball "many times."[30] In June 1913, a reporter felt his "sulking" actually cost the Naps a game.[31] His downcast attitude was obvious.

So far, for Jackson, there was no sulking, no apparent miscues, and nothing he had personally done to raise suspicion. His role in the active fix was minimal, but Joe still wanted the money he was promised. When Gandil failed to produce the cash, he was left with very few options. It wasn't like he could complain to a reporter, and he certainly was in no position to go over Chick's head and converse with the higher-ups. Jackson was out on a vine with his compatriots and at the mercy of those unscrupulous characters he agreed to join. But facing Gandil and Swede Risberg with any type of aggressiveness was also looking for trouble, as both were imposing tough guys. And that was a situation Jackson was going to avoid. Needless to say, the intimidation shown by Gandil and Risberg was going to prevent anyone from running off and ratting on the deal. For the time being, each of the players involved was supposed to lay low and wait it out.

But Jackson didn't know that Gandil had collected $10,000 from Burns and Attell after the second game, just before leaving Cincinnati.[32] And he wouldn't see a dime of it. Additionally, Burns passed along Attell's orders, indicating he wanted the Sox to win the third game to improve the overall odds for the Series. According to the testimony of Burns in 1921, Gandil and those privy to the inside information agreed, but once back in Chicago, Chick notified Burns that the third game was going to have the same result as the first two. That, in turn, motivated Burns, his pal Billy Maharg (who had been with him on the scam from the start), and Attell to bet heavy on Cincinnati, assured that the Sox were going to throw the game. However, Burns later realized Chick had no intention of losing the third game. In a double-cross fashion, as a way to punish the gamblers for not paying up, the Sox went forward and beat the Reds, 3–0.[33]

That version was told by Burns himself, who felt personally deceived because of Gandil's suspected lie. Yet in 1920, Jackson claimed the crooked members of the club really tried to lose the third game, and Chicago won only because the honest Sox stepped up.[34] If this was true, then Gandil never lied to Burns and didn't double-cross the gamblers purposefully. It was just the result of the chance involved in such a scheme. With a number of nonparticipants actively trying to win, the result was never guaranteed. Going back to the third game itself, the honest Sox were more enthusiastic than ever to win, and Kid Gleason was determined to have his men in the right frame of mind before the contest began.

Shano Collins later remembered: "When we reported at the grounds, Gleason called us into the clubhouse, chased out the trainer and clubhouse boy, and then read the riot act. He told us that the word was going around that some of the Chicago White Sox had sold out the Series and that it was up to us to throttle the rumor. This talk put us on edge, and we went in against the Reds to give them a real battle. Little Dick Kerr pitched this game, and it was the first of the Series we won. We never knew, Kerr never dreamed that he and four loyal players were downing Cincinnati and half of his own team. The alleged testimony of Jackson and others has stated how little Dick won in spite of treachery by his mates. And even at that it took a couple of lucky breaks to get us the decision."

Rookie Dickey Kerr was the star of the day. He held the Reds scoreless with his pinpoint control, and the Sox offense came up with three runs to push Chicago to its first victory of the Series. Strikingly, the team was in a fighting mood, utterly refusing to relent on its path to victory. Eddie Collins nearly came to blows with Reds utilityman Jimmy Smith, and only Gleason prevented a fistfight. "Then Jackson and [pitcher Ray] Fisher had a row because Fisher shot one at Joe's bean and Joe bunted one toward first base, daring Fisher to go over and cover the bag," Gleason explained. "Joe was mad enough to have spiked him, too, but nothing came of that."[35] Altogether, Jackson went 2-for-3 with a run in the game, including base hits to start the second and sixth innings. He eventually scored in the second but was caught trying to steal second in the sixth. Joe had another opportunity in the third inning with two men on but errantly popped up his bunt attempt to first baseman Jake Daubert.[36]

If Gandil and his allies in the fix consciously decided to win behind "busher" Kerr in the third game, either Jackson was left out of the plan or refused to admit it based on his later revelations.[37] But looking at the box score, it was obvious those players tied to the conspiracy were more motivated to win than they previously demonstrated. They contributed five of the seven Sox hits, two of the three RBIs, and all three runs. Gandil himself was responsible for both of those RBIs, and

Risberg added a triple.[38] Burns and Attell learned very quickly that the players had a measure of recourse if they didn't honor their end of the deal. As for Kid Gleason, he was thrilled by what appeared to be a full renewal of his team's unity and drive to win. Fans and local sportswriters were also revitalized by the victory, and with the usually competent Cicotte returning to the slab for Game Four, hopes were high in Chicago.

But Game Four was a lifeless effort by the Sox players. They compiled just three hits off Cincinnati pitcher Jimmy Ring and were unable to score, while the Reds garnered five hits and two runs. Cicotte, instead of building upon what Kerr had started, shamelessly disappointed, and his fifth-inning performance was the turning point of the contest. The madness started with one out and Pat Duncan at the plate. Duncan hit a grounder up the middle and Cicotte made a nice stop. He rushed his throw to Gandil at first, and the peg was way off target, allowing Duncan to reach second. Larry Kopf followed with a single to left field. Jackson made a great stop and unflinchingly threw toward home plate to prevent Duncan from scoring. Surprisingly, Cicotte stepped in front of the ball to cut it off, and it ricocheted off his glove for his second error of the inning. Duncan scored on the play and Kopf continued on to second. Greasy Neale proceeded to add to Chicago's misery by smashing a double over the head of Jackson in left, scoring Kopf, and giving the Reds a 2–0 lead.[39]

"The . . . game was another upset," Shano Collins explained. "I think it was here that our players really began to be convinced that there was something really wrong. We were feeling rather downcast that night. I don't mind saying right now that some of us began to pay a little more attention to the stories that were circulating more widely every hour."[40] Jackson went 1-for-4, and his double to start the second inning initiated a potential rally, but Cicotte drew the third out with the bases loaded. After the contest, Lefty Williams visited his [Jackson's] room at the Lexington Hotel in Chicago's South Loop and delivered $5,000 in cash, compiled of "mostly fifties."[41] This would be the only crooked money of the entire conspiracy that Jackson would see and was but one-fourth of his promised amount. Williams was actually given $10,000 but kept half, as it was the only cash he'd seen to that point, as well.[42]

Jackson was bought and partially paid for by gamblers at that juncture, and nothing in history could change that ugly truth. Prior to being paid, he was definitely complicit and possibly committed to doing his part in the throwing of games. But, after cash changed hands, the famous "Shoeless Joe" was unequivocally stained by the corruptness of the 1919 baseball scandal. According to Jackson's Grand Jury testimony, Katie first learned about the fix that same night following the fourth game, and she "thought it was an awful thing to do."[43] Nobody knows what was said between them in their hotel room that night, but it is likely Joe gained a better perspective of what he'd involved himself in from his wife than at any previous time. No one on the team was going to be the straight shooter that Katie was, and none of his co-conspirators were looking out for his best interests like she had always done. It is within good probability that Katie informed Joe just how much trouble he could be in for his faulty thinking.

Incidentally, touching upon Jackson's mind-set a little more, it must be noted that Cincinnati applied a heavy dose of psychological warfare during the Series. "The Reds were primed to abuse and insult certain Sox players with the idea of getting them angry," Hugh Fullerton later wrote. Twenty-four-year-old utility player Jimmy Smith, "a hot head and fighter at heart," was a base coach for the Reds and the lead instigator. He worked on Eddie Collins relentlessly, nearly draw-ing the Sox captain into a physical altercation. Fullerton noted that Jackson was targeted for abuse, as well.[44] Of course, Jackson was thin-skinned about his wartime duty with Harlan and Hollingsworth, and the Reds took advantage of that unique sensitivity. As the *Indianapolis Star* reported, "The Reds . . . annoyed Joe Jackson intensely by con-stantly referring to the shipyards league."[45] It seemed that part of his life was something he'd never live down.

With the Reds ahead three games to one, the Series appeared near-ly out of reach for the Sox, but Chicago fans yearned for a turnaround. They wanted to see the real club of 1919, a team many people con-sidered to be the best ever constructed. Things didn't improve in the fifth game at Comiskey Park on October 6, the day after a Sunday rainout. The Sox were ineffectual behind the pitching of Lefty Wil-liams, achieving three hits and no runs against the mastery of Reds pitcher Hod Eller, who struck out nine in a 5–0 victory. The loss left the Sox players (at least those who were trying) nearly comatose in a Series they were supposed to win.[46] Jackson was completely shut down by the right-handed Eller and went 0-for-4. Twice he went to the plate with men in scoring position, and twice he failed to bring them home.

The Series returned to Cincinnati for Game Six on October 7, and it was do or die for the Sox. Kid Gleason called upon Kerr again, and Dickey pitched 10 innings of hard-nosed baseball. In the end, the Sox won, 5–4, and Chicago was able to live another day. Jackson went 2-for-4 on the day with a run and an RBI, and contributed to big rallies in the sixth and tenth innings. Twice, though, he was doubled up on the baselines after the defense made difficult catches—once by Edd Roush in the eighth and the other by Larry Kopf in the tenth. In the fourth inning, Joe made a spectacular defensive play of his own by snaring a fly by Jake Daubert and launched a perfect throw to catcher Ray Schalk to nail Morrie Rath at the plate.[47] Jackson garnered another two hits the following day in Game Seven, helping the Sox beat the Reds, 4–1. This time, Joe's clutch hitting drove in runs in both the first and third innings, and Cicotte went the distance to halt Cincinnati's charge for a fifth and final Series victory.[48]

There has been ample speculation that dissatisfied Sox conspirators decided to forge ahead after the fifth game (Cincinnati was leading, 4–1) and make a serious comeback attempt to win the Series outright. The wins in Games Six and Seven were indicative of a team effort, and Cicotte's performance in the latter contest was more in tune with his regular season showing. Gamblers who'd bet on Cincinnati going all the way were dismayed by the sudden burst of energy displayed by Chicago, and it was alleged that Lefty Williams was menaced by a mysterious man prior to Game Eight to ensure the Sox would lose. If it did indeed happen, the threat to Williams and perhaps to his wife, as well, was cause enough for Lefty to pitch about as poor a performance as a major leaguer could. On October 9, 1919, at Comiskey Park, Williams lasted but part of the first inning and gave up four runs on four hits.

Jackson provided some excitement in the third inning by hitting the first home run of the Series into the right-field bleachers. He also added a double in the eighth that scored two runs. In the bottom of the ninth, with two outs and two men on, and the Sox trailing by five runs, Jackson grounded to second baseman Morrie Rath to end the game and the Series.[49] The Cincinnati Reds won, 10–5, and captured the 1919 World Series title. Following the game, Kid Gleason told a reporter: "The Reds beat the greatest ball team that ever went into a World's Series. But it wasn't the real White Sox. They played baseball for me only a couple or three of the eight days. Something was wrong.

I didn't like the betting odds. I wish no one had ever bet a dollar on the team."[50]

As could be expected, there was a certain amount of "resentment [by members of the Sox] toward some of the players who did not perform up to expectations," as observed by a writer for the *Chicago Daily Tribune*.[51] The failure of these men to execute their ordinary level of play made them possible suspects in the growing rumors of a Series fix. Of those involved, Chick Gandil batted .233, Happy Felsch .192, Swede Risberg .080, and the Sox defense committed an uncharacteristic 12 errors in eight games. So uncharacteristic, as they had made 176 errors as a team in 1919, which was the second lowest in the American League that season.

For Joe Jackson, he played well, carrying the highest batting average of the Sox regulars (.375, 12-for-32), and the most hits (12—a World Series record), runs (5), RBIs (6), and highest slugging percentage (.563). He also made no errors. Captain Eddie Collins, who was one of the Series disappointments, acknowledged Joe's work in the *Chicago Daily News*, stating that Jackson "maintained his reputation with the stick." Ray Schalk agreed, noting, "Joe Jackson hit as hard as he did during the season, or even a little better."[52]

Writer Oscar C. Reichow added, "Jackson certainly demonstrated that a World's Series makes little difference to him. He played up to his standard."[53] However, not everyone felt a high average was representative of a player truly performing on the level. "Some of the men accused of crookedness have pointed to the fact that they hit well up in the averages for this Series, and that their fielding was well-nigh faultless," said Shano Collins. "I won't argue with them along this line. I will only state that very few of these hits were made at the proper time and that errors were made just when they cost the most."[54] Jackson failed to produce a total of eight times when men were on base, seven of them with runners in scoring position. These facts are not definitive proof of Jackson's contributions to the fix, but it does highlight other mitigating factors of his Series play. In truth, no one to this day can say for sure whether Jackson played honest and true baseball during the 1919 World Series. All we have are the stats, and they only tell part of the story.

NOTES

1. *Boston Post*, October 23, 1920, p. 9.
2. *Sports Illustrated*, September 17, 1956.
3. *San Francisco Chronicle*, August 25, 1912.
4. *Washington Times*, May 24, 1918, p. 18.
5. *Chicago American*, September 3, 1919.
6. *The Sporting News*, February 20, 1919, p. 1.
7. *The Sporting News*, January 23, 1919, p. 1.
8. *Chicago Daily News*, September 24, 1919, p. 1.
9. Some fans in Chicago "hissed and booed" the Sox for their performance. *Chicago Daily News*, September 29, 1919, p. 1.
10. *Chicago Daily Tribune*, September 21, 1919, p. A1.
11. *The Sporting News*, August 28, 1919, p. 1.
    Robbins also stated, "Probably not in the history of baseball has there been a greater money team than the White Sox."
12. *New York Evening World*, September 29, 1920, p. 7.
13. *New York Tribune*, September 30, 1920, p. 2.
14. *Chicago Daily Tribune*, July 8, 1919, p. 17.
15. *New York Tribune*, September 30, 1920, p. 2.
16. Jackson talked at length about the "promises" made him before the Grand Jury. Joe Jackson Grand Jury Testimony Transcript, Bart Garrison Agricultural Museum of South Carolina, Pendleton, South Carolina.
17. Jesse Barnes of the New York Giants won 25 games in 1919. Cincinnati had the top three pitchers in terms of win-loss percentage in Dutch Ruether (.760), Slim Sallee (.750), and Ray Fisher (.737). Baseball-reference.com.
18. *Chicago Daily News*, September 30, 1919, p. 2.
19. *Chicago American*, August 4, 1919.
20. *Chicago Daily News*, September 11, 1919, p. 1.
21. *Chicago Daily Tribune*, October 2, 1919, p. 22.

22. *Chicago Daily Tribune*, October 2, 1919, p. 22.
23. *Boston Post*, November 27, 1920, p. 12.
24. Joe Jackson Grand Jury Testimony Transcript, Bart Garrison Agricultural Museum of South Carolina, Pendleton, South Carolina.
25. Jackson reportedly told his friend Lefty Williams that it was a "crooked deal" after the first day and felt Gandil was not being honest with them. Joe Jackson Grand Jury Testimony Transcript, Bart Garrison Agricultural Museum of South Carolina, Pendleton, South Carolina. According to one account, Felsch was, in fact, paid $5,000 after the first game in Cincinnati. *Milwaukee Evening Sentinel*, October 1, 1920, p. 18.
26. *Boston Post*, November 27, 1920, p. 12.
27. *Chicago Daily Tribune*, October 3, 1919, p. 22.
28. *Boston Post*, November 27, 1920, p. 12.
29. Joe Jackson Grand Jury Testimony Transcript, Bart Garrison Agricultural Museum of South Carolina, Pendleton, South Carolina.
30. *Cleveland Leader*, December 21, 1912, p. 7.
31. *Anaconda Standard*, June 22, 1913, p. 23.
32. *New York Times*, July 21, 1921, p. 9.
33. Ibid.
34. *New York Tribune*, September 30, 1920, p. 2.
35. *Chicago Daily Tribune*, October 4, 1919, pp. 17–18.
36. Ibid.
37. There were claims that Gandil and his cronies refused to win for "bush leaguer" Dickey Kerr. However, there were allegations that this crew met for a special meeting before the third game, ultimately deciding to win and double-cross the gamblers.
38. Baseball-reference.com.
39. *Chicago Daily Tribune*, October 5, 1919, p. A2.
40. *Boston Post*, November 27, 1920, p. 12.
41. Joe Jackson Grand Jury Testimony Transcript, Bart Garrison Agricultural Museum of South Carolina, Pendleton, South Carolina.
42. *New York Tribune*, September 30, 1920, p. 2.
43. Joe Jackson Grand Jury Testimony Transcript, Bart Garrison Agricultural Museum of South Carolina, Pendleton, South Carolina. Jackson incorrectly told the jury that he was paid the same night they were traveling back to Cincinnati. Games four and five were both in Chicago.
44. *The Sporting News*, October 30, 1919, p. 3.
45. *Indianapolis Star*, October 14, 1919, p. 14.
46. *Chicago Daily Tribune*, October 7, 1919, pp. 21–22.
47. *Chicago Daily Tribune*, October 8, 1919, p. 18.
48. *Chicago Daily Tribune*, October 9, 1919, pp. 21–22.
49. *Chicago Daily Tribune*, October 10, 1919, pp. 19–20.
50. Ibid.

51. Ibid.
52. *Chicago Daily News*, October 10, 1919, p. 2.
53. *Chicago Daily News*, October 11, 1919, p. 2.
54. *Boston Post*, November 27, 1920, p. 12.

PART TWO

MEMORABLE MOMENTS AND PERSONALITIES

CHAPTER 6

HAVING A CAREER DAY

STAN FISCHLER

FROM THIRD-STRING CATCHER
TO FIRST-STRING SPY

Morris (Moe) Berg hardly had a distinguished baseball career. If anything, his only claim to diamond fame was longevity. The catcher from Newark, NJ, lasted in the bigs from 1923 to 1939, playing for the Brooklyn Dodgers, Chicago White Sox, Cleveland Indians, Washington Senators, and finally, the Boston Red Sox.

It was in the realm of spying that Berg was exceptionally successful. Working for Uncle Sam when he wasn't behind the plate—among other feats—Berg laid the groundwork for General Jimmy Doolittle's thirty-second bombing of Tokyo in 1942.

In another instance, Berg was responsible for British Prime Minister Winston Churchill's support of Marshal Josip Broz Tito's Nazi-resistance group over Commander Dragoljub Mihalovic's Serbian forces. Parachuting into Yugoslavia at age forty-one, Berg took stock of Marshal Tito's scrappy partisans and reported back to Churchill.

It was Moe's impressive status as a polyglot that led him to espionage. His pharmacist father, Bernard, taught him Hebrew and Yiddish, and he learned Latin, Greek, and French in high school. At Princeton University, Berg added Spanish, Italian, German, and Sanskrit to his repertoire, and after studying in Paris and then Columbia Law School, he picked up Hungarian, Portuguese, Arabic, Japanese, Korean, Chinese languages, and more Indian languages. In all, he boasted knowledge of fifteen languages, not to mention the various regional dialects.

Berg began playing baseball at age four, but his stern father disapproved of the ball game and refused to watch his son play, even when Moe played shortstop for Princeton. After college, Berg went on to play for the Brooklyn Robins (later the Dodgers) as a backup catcher. His baseball career was mediocre at best, but he was venerated by sportswriters, fellow players, and fans alike for his intellectual brilliance.

Japanese baseball fans were no exception; they were thrilled when Berg was, somewhat unexpectedly and, in light of his position as a third-string catcher, somewhat undeservedly, chosen to accompany MLB greats, such as Babe Ruth and Lou Gehrig, on an All-Star tour of Japan in 1934. Yet, unbeknownst to all—save for key U.S. government officials—Berg was not on tour to promote the sport of baseball.

Instead, the Japanese-speaking Princeton grad was instructed to film key features of Tokyo for use in General Doolittle's 1942 raid.

Berg was also tasked with determining how close the Nazis were to constructing the world's first atomic bomb. With famed physicist Werner Heisenberg at the forefront of the German nuclear energy project, the stakes were getting higher by the day.

Posing as a Swiss graduate student, Moe Berg sat in the front row of the Nobel Laureate's lecture with a pistol and a cyanide pill in his pocket. His task: assess the Nazi's progress on building a nuclear bomb,

Moe Berg as a member of the Boston Red Sox in 1933. *AP Photo.*

and if he judged that they were close to achieving their goal, he was to shoot Heisenberg and swallow the cyanide pill. Fortunately for all, Berg's assessment came back negative.

After the war, Berg found himself out of a job. He occasionally received intelligence assignments, but always saw himself as a ballplayer. When asked, "Why are you wasting your talent?" Berg responded, "I'd rather be a ballplayer than a Justice on the U.S. Supreme Court."

Moe Berg was awarded the Medal of Merit—America's highest honor for a civilian in wartime. But Berg refused to accept it, as he could not tell people about his exploits. After his death, his sister accepted the medal, and it hangs in the Baseball Hall of Fame, in Cooperstown, NY.

STAN MUSIAL SHOWS WHY HE IS "THE MAN"

When Stan Musial's name comes up for discussion among those who know baseball's history best, the first of his feats that comes to mind is the man's seven National League batting championships.

His clutch hitting—especially at Brooklyn's Ebbets Field—inspired Dodger fans to nickname him "the Man."

More specifically, when Musial walked up to the batter's box at the Flatbush ballpark, Dodger fans were likely to murmur, "Here comes the man!" A writer covering the Dodgers-Cardinals game one day overheard the comment, and from that point on, Musial was "Stan the Man."

As effective as Musial was in Brooklyn, his best day as a home run hitter took place on May 2, 1954, at Busch Stadium in St. Louis. On that day, in a doubleheader against the New York Giants, Musial hit five home runs.

Stan "The Man" Musial belted five home runs in a doubleheader against the New York Giants in 1954. *AP Photo.*

Musial had three homers in the Cards' first fourteen games, and there was little reason to suspect that he would break out in a rash of four-baggers this time, particularly with Johnny Antonelli, one of the league's top southpaws, pitching the first game for the Giants.

His third and final home run in the first game was a game-winning blow. The Cards won, 10–6, behind Stan's three-home-run performance.

Manager Leo Durocher of the Giants nominated Don Liddle, another lefty, to work the nightcap. In Musial's second plate appearance of the second game, he was finally retired: the first time he was sent back to the dugout all day.

Knuckleballer Hoyt Wilhelm was on the mound for the Giants when Musial came to the plate. With one man on base, Musial connected again, hammering a ball over the pavilion roof for his fourth homer of the day.

Then in the seventh inning, Stan punished another ball over the right field roof. This narrowed the Giants' lead to one run. The Cards could not get another run across and split the doubleheader.

In eight official trips to the plate, Musial collected five home runs, one single, nine runs batted in, and twenty-one total bases. He set a Major League record with his five homers in the twin bill and tied the record for homers in two consecutive games.

ONE HAND, NO HITS—HOW CAN THAT HAPPEN?

Pitching in the Major Leagues is tough. Pitching a no-hitter is even tougher. Pitching a no-hitter, having only one hand——now that is undoubtedly the toughest task.

Left-hander Jim Abbott was born without a right hand: only a stump above the wrist at the end of his right arm. Abbott embraced the card he was dealt, though. While he could've given in to his limitations, he refused to bask in self-pity and instead chose to take a different route.

"I didn't want to be defined by a disability," Abbott once said.

His drive to compete and his love for sports made up for the physical parts he lacked. At a young age, one of the sports that attracted him the most was baseball. The only question became: how could he pitch, let alone play, with only one hand?

Abbott found the answer.

"I learned to play baseball like most kids, playing catch with my dad in the front yard. The only difference was that we had to come up with a method to throw and catch with the same hand. What we came up with is basically what I continued to do my whole life."

Abbott practiced by throwing a ball against a brick wall, switching his glove off and on. When the ball bounced back to him, he flipped the glove to his left hand, ready to field.

He introduced that method in Little League, when at eleven years old, he pitched a no-hitter in his first game. He stuck with it through high school, finding further success as both a pitcher and hitter. At the University of Michigan, Abbott became one of the most talked-about baseball players in the country, winning the Sullivan Award one year, honoring the country's most outstanding amateur athlete. His nearly flawless winning percentage during college (he won twenty-six of thirty-four games he pitched for Michigan) earned him a spot on Team USA in the 1987 Pan American Games and in the 1988 Olympics.

The best, of course, was yet to come.

Abbott made it to the Major Leagues in 1989, remarkably enough, without pitching a single game in the minors. He had defied all odds and broke into the highest professional level, despite what he lacked. In his rookie season with the California Angels, he finished fifth in the American League Rookie of the Year voting. In 1991, he won eighteen games for the Angels and finished third in voting for the Cy Young Award.

To make his storybook journal even more miraculous, Abbott achieved the highlight of his career in Yankee pinstripes at perhaps baseball's most holy of grounds, Yankee Stadium.

Abbott's first season with the New York Yankees came in 1993. By September 4, 1993, he boasted only a less-than-stellar record of nine wins and eleven losses. He took the mound that day against the Cleveland Indians. Even when the game entered the eighth inning and Abbott had yet to allow a hit, the prospects of a no-hitter may have been doubtful to some. Besides, Abbott flirted with a no-hitter into the eighth that same year back in May, before losing it.

But, the eighth came and went. Eight innings passed without an Indians hit.

The Yankees held a comfortable 4–0 lead into the ninth inning, so the win was the furthest thing from fans' minds. They were anxiously hoping for the first Yankee Stadium no-hitter in ten years, and they got their wish. Abbott retired the Indians in the ninth, completing a no-hitter and adding to his laundry list of accomplishments.

Jim Abbott did not have an exceptional Major League career, but he did have his share of exceptional moments. From practicing his un-orthodox pitching method against a brick wall to his no-hitter, Abbott found success at each level along the way. His perseverance, combined with his dedication and willpower, has made Abbott one of the most inspirational figures in sports.

Jim Abbott celebrates his no-hitter against the Cleveland Indians as teammate Wade Boggs runs to congratulate him. *AP Photo/Bebeto Matthews.*

THE MOST SENSATIONAL GAME EVER PITCHED

In the history of professional baseball (that's well over one hundred thousand games, but who's counting?), only twenty-three perfect games have been tossed. One is thrown roughly every 4,400 starts—give or take a couple hundred.

If you're a fan of percentages, that means every time you watch a baseball game, you have about .023 percent chance of seeing a perfecto—the expression "one-in-a-million" quite literally applies here.

While a perfect game is rare enough, on September 9, 1965, Sandy Koufax and Bob Hendley of the Cubs hooked up for a pitchers' duel, the likes of which had never been seen before, and hasn't been seen since a 1–0 victory for Koufax's Dodgers in which two men—no really, just two—reached base (Lou Johnson, on a walk and a double), a record for offensive futility that still stands today.

Koufax's exploits alone would be enough to qualify this game as amongst the best ever pitched. The splendid southpaw turned in the most dominating performance of a career full of them, striking out fourteen—including the final six—as he spun his first and only perfect game.

The fourteen Ks was a record for a perfect game that has since been tied by Matt Cain, but unlike Koufax, Cain can't say he struck out Hall of Famer Ernie Banks three times when he took his turn at making history—or had to find a way to retire another Hall of Fame Cubbie, Ron Santo.

Koufax's perfecto is also remarkable for one other reason—a lack of a memorable defensive play. It seems like in every perfect game or no-hitter, there's at least one close call—it could be early, it could be late—but there's always at least one play where the man on the mound

Sandy Koufax struck out 14 batters in his perfect game against the Chicago Cubs in 1965. It was the fourth no-hitter of his career. *AP Photo.*

needs some help from his friends. Not so with Koufax. Scour as many accounts of the game as you want, but there's nary a description of a single hard-hit ball off of Koufax on that fateful day.

Despite Koufax's phenomenal exploits, it takes two to tango. For a game truly to be the greatest ever pitched, the man toeing the rubber for the opposing side needs to be up for the challenge, as well—and all Bob Hendley did was turn in the performance of a lifetime. Hendley surrendered just one run—it was unearned, scored on a throwing error by his catcher—one hit, and two base runners all game long. In fact, Hendley carried a no-no of his own into the seventh and only lost it on what is described in all accounts as a bloop double by Lou Johnson, who, remarkably, was the only player to reach base for either side that game (he did so twice).

There has never, in the history of baseball, been a double no-hitter, but in September '65, Koufax and Hendley came as close as anyone ever has and turned in a pair of performances that stand the test of time.

WHY DID THREE CRUCIAL PLAYERS IN THE 1947 WORLD SERIES NEVER PLAY ANOTHER BIG LEAGUE GAME?

In 1947, heated rivals—the New York Yankees and the Brooklyn Dodgers—faced off in the World Series.

But the Series would mark the final major league games for three key players. Can you recall any of their names?

In Game Four, Bill Bevens of the Bombers and Harry Taylor of the Brooks squared off at Ebbets Field. Taylor was quickly knocked out of the game and replaced by Hal Gregg. But Bevens rolled mightily along, allowing one run, ten walks, a wild pitch, and incredibly, not a single hit through eight innings.

In the bottom of the ninth, Carl Furillo of the Dodgers was walked with one out. Al Gionfriddo was sent in to run for Furillo. With two outs, pinch hitter Pistol Pete Reiser, who was suffering from a lame ankle, stepped into the batter's box. Reiser was intentionally walked to bring up weak-hitting Eddie Stanky. But he never made it to the plate.

Cookie Lavagetto (left) poses with Floyd "Bill" Bevens the day after Lavagetto's pinch-hit double broke up Bevens's no-hitter and drove in the tying and winning runs to lead the Brooklyn Dodgers over the New York Yankees in Game Four of the 1947 World Series. *AP Photo.*

Stanky was replaced by ancient third baseman Cookie Lavagetto, who responded with a line drive that bounced off the right field wall to score Gionfriddo, as well as Eddie Miksis, who had been sent in to run for Reiser.

Lavagetto's double won the game for Brooklyn, 3–2. Bevens had lost a no-hitter as well as a World Series one-hitter in the bottom of the ninth.

Although both appeared again over the course of the Series, neither Bevens nor Lavagetto would play in another regular-season game.

Bevens had had a poor year and decided to conclude his four-year career after the Series. Meanwhile, Lavagetto was winding down a fourteen-year major league career, ten of them with the Dodgers. He retired with a tidy .300 lifetime average.

Gionfriddo, the third man in the group, also factored significantly in the outcome of the Series. His shining moment came in Game Six at Yankee Stadium. With two on and two out in the bottom of the sixth, Joe DiMaggio drove a deep fly ball that appeared to be headed for the bleachers, until Gionfriddo flagged it down at the 415-foot sign in front of the bullpen.

As the stoical DiMaggio rounded first, he saw the ball slam into Gionfriddo's glove. The Yankee Clipper then betrayed visible emotion for one of the few times in his career, kicking at the dirt before returning to the bench. The catch saved the sixth game and kept Dodger hurler Joe Hatten alive.

Gionfriddo was concluding a four-year Major League career, which included stints in Pittsburgh and Brooklyn. In thirty-seven games with the Brooks in 1947, he hit just .177. But his catch helped the Dodgers tie the Series and force Game Seven. He was never heard from again.

The Yankees ultimately prevailed in the seventh game as Gionfriddo, Bevens, and Lavagetto saw their names inscribed in the books before departing from the majors forever.

CHAPTER 7

DRAFTING JIM THOME AND MANNY RAMÍREZ

GEORGE CHRISTIAN PAPPAS

SCOUTING REPORT

From the Desk of Tom Couston

"Inside-out swing at this point . . . willingly uses the opposite field. . . . Excellent power potential if he learns to turn on the ball . . . could easily add weight and muscle to 200-pound frame. Works hard at defense, but may not have the range to stay at third base. . . . High-character guy. Comes from strong blue-collar family."

If it wasn't for Chet Montgomery acting on the gut instincts of his Midwest-area scout, baseball might have never been introduced to one of its most prolific home-run hitters. It's something that even the slugger admits. The scout was Tom Couston,[1] and the boy

---

[1] Couston's last name is modified from his family's Greek surname, Kostopanagiotis.

he saw on a scouting trip to Limestone Community High School in Peoria County, Illinois, was not unlike any of the thousands of other teenaged players he had seen as he scoured dusty ball fields around Middle America for talent. Jim Thome had dreams of becoming a big leaguer just like the rest of them.

"Jimmy doesn't forget where he came from," says Couston. It's true enough that the scout was invited to sit with Thome's father at U.S. Cellular Field in Chicago to watch as the slugger hit career home run No. 500 on September 16, 2007.

The largest city on the Illinois River, Peoria is so representative of the average American city that it has been referenced historically as a standard for mainstream Midwestern culture. The question "Will it play in Peoria?" was so often asked about acts on the vaudeville theater circuit at the turn of the twentieth century that the meaning of the phrase was eventually generalized to address the appeals of the American people as a whole. It's only fitting that Jim, the youngest of Chuck Jr. and Joyce Thome's five children, came from a pedigree of softball players enshrined in the Greater Peoria Sports Hall of Fame to honor the multigenerational achievements on the diamond by his father, Grandfather Chuck Sr., Uncle Art, and Aunt Carolyn. By the time he was eight, Jim announced to his mother that he was never going to work and that he was going to play baseball in the big leagues.

If he couldn't round up the neighborhood kids for a game, Jim picked up an aluminum bat and hit white rocks from the driveway of the family home. He tried smacking the rocks the same way his idol, Chicago Cubs long-ball specialist Dave Kingman, crushed baseballs. Jim grew up watching the Cubs on WGN and lauded "Kong" for his tape-measure home runs that often soared past the bleachers and beyond the friendly confines of Wrigley Field, crashing through the windows of the apartments facing the ballpark along Waveland Avenue with reckless disregard.

Jim once tried to get an autograph from Kingman when his dad took him to his first Cubs game. They drove about 150 miles from Chicago and had seats near the dugout. After Kingman snubbed his request during batting practice, the nine-year-old Thome vaulted over a wall, found his way through the dugout, and headed toward the club-house, determined to meet his favorite slugger. Barry Foote, the Cubs' catcher, stopped Jim and returned him to his father, but not before he handed the boy a baseball signed by some of his teammates. The brief encounter in the dugout only reinforced the idea that Jim wanted nothing more than to become a major leaguer.

Thome had not yet filled out his 6-foot-4-inch, 250-pound frame when Couston saw him for the first time in high school. Jim was lanky and had a sunken chest. Just by looking at his limbs and torso, the scout could tell he still had room to develop into a burly power hitter. Jim's older brothers were physical guys, and their father was even bigger.

Jim's time running to first base turned away some of the first scouts who evaluated him. It took him almost five seconds to lumber the ninety feet to the bag.[2] He would swing so hard that he often got tied up in the batter's box . . . but that did not scare Couston. Apart from clocking him at 6.8 seconds (a strong average time) in the 60-yard dash, the scout had other indicators to prove that Thome was ath-letic. He was the leading scorer on his high school basketball team, an All-State guard who put up 36 points when Limestone won its league title in triple overtime. Sure, he didn't have the first-step quickness to be a shortstop, but his glove was decent and he threw well enough to

---

[2] A time of 4.2 seconds to first base for a left-handed batter is considered average. Five seconds is inferior.

keep his bat in the lineup and not be a liability in the field. That factor would be helpful to any suitor, because Jim's bat would certainly be his most intriguing draw. But at that time, there were no suitors. Couston heard that Thome was going to play baseball in junior college, something the scout thought would benefit the young player; therefore, Jim's name was not called on draft day in 1988.

A year passed before Couston saw Thome again, in April of 1989. There were a handful of scouts on hand, but they had all gathered to see another shortstop play against Illinois Central College. Even Couston had come to see the other team's prospect but spotted Thome and recognized him as the strong kid from Peoria whom he had seen the previous spring. The other scouts paid no attention to him, probably still thinking he was too slow and awkward to be a shortstop. Couston, on the other hand, saw much improvement in his game.

Thome already showed signs that he was growing. He was still only eighteen and would have additional time for his body to mature even further. Moreover, he was beginning to look like a major-league hitter in the batter's box. He seemed to have a good idea of the strike zone and exhibited a total sense of control over his body, with enough strength in his arms from his elbows to his wrists to make solid contact. Most kids who swung that hard would often hit the bottom of the baseball and make weaker contact.

The ball also seemed to rise a little off Thome's bat when he connected on pitches. His swing was still occasionally long, which would have deterred some other scouts, but his bat speed and contact made up for it. The stroke was becoming smoother, more compact and plenty more powerful. *With some more at bats in pro ball, he will develop wrists so strong that he'll finally have loft; the final dimension to becoming a power hitter and regularly blast towering shots,* Couston thought.

Thome made four outs in as many plate appearances that day, but, as the scout noted, they came off his bat with such force that they could have decapitated the infielders. Impressed, Couston decided that he would approach him after the game. He walked up to the coach and asked him to send over his shortstop to talk, but the coach brought over the wrong kid. *Jeez, nobody must want to talk to this guy.* Thome eventually came over, and to avoid tipping off any of the remaining

Jim Thome hit 612 home runs during his career, 263 as a member of the Cleveland Indians. *AP Photo/Ron Schwane.*

scouts lingering by the field that he was interested, Couston resorted to one of his favorite tricks. He instructed Thome to keep his back to him. The scout did the same.

"I want to talk to you, but don't look me in the eye," Couston said.

This confused Thome. He thought he might have done something wrong, but followed the scout's directions and started looking around the ball field.

"Do you want to play professional baseball?" Couston asked.

Thome turned his attention back to the scout.

"Quit lookin' at me!" he snapped.

Thome immediately turned back around and nodded, "Yes, sir, I do."

That was the scout's cue to introduce himself.

"My name is Tom Couston and I'm a scout from the Indians. I'm gonna come back and see you. I'm not gonna talk to you, but I'll be talking to you before the draft."

That was it. The exchange couldn't have lasted any longer, or else the other scouts might have caught on. Thome still laughs about Couston's sly scouting tactics more than twenty years later. But at the onset of his major-league journey, he was just pleased to be considered as one of the club's future draft selections.

* * *

"There are actually two jobs in baseball with a paper trail for success in the front office. One's the GM and one's the scouting director. It's written in blood, and that's essentially what John Hart and I were faced with."

—Mickey White, former Indians amateur scouting director

Mickey White was forty years old when he took over for Chet Montgomery to oversee the amateur draft in the United States and the Indians' international focus in Venezuela, Panama, and the Dominican Republic. He had flown out to Cleveland in September of 1990 to meet with John Hart about the position while at the time serving as an East Coast cross-checker for the Seattle Mariners. Mickey and his wife were invited back for a game in Hank Peters's luxury box, and he got a phone call with the job offer the day after he returned home. He moved his wife and three kids to Strongsville, a suburb southwest of Cleveland, in January of 1991 to begin work.

There was a sense of familiarity about Cleveland and its people that hit home for Mickey, who traces his roots back to Pittsburgh.

"The people were the same, they just wore different colors for the football games," he recalls. "That's how it was when you were dealing with people from the quote-unquote Rust Belt cities. They're all kind of same, very little bulls**t, tell-it-to-your-face kind of people."

He had quite a surprise when he learned his new next-door neighbor had gone to Kent State, where he was a teammate of Steelers great Jack Lambert. The two immediately became friends.

But the change at the head of the scouting department wasn't the only difference for the Indians as the organization prepared for the 1991 amateur draft. Cleveland's back-to-back failures in the first rounds of '89 and '90 prompted Hank Peters to make an announcement when his scouts met at the 1990 Winter Meetings. His decree: Tom Giordano would accompany any scout before signing the club's next No. 1 pick. He didn't want them to mess this next one up, and for good reason. The Indians had been eyeing their eventual top pick for four years, and he was the kind of kid, as scout Joe DeLucca put it, that "you only see once in your life."

* * *

Joe DeLucca will deny any claim that he *discovered* Manny Ramírez. Everybody knew about Manny when he played ball as a teenager in northern Manhattan's Washington Heights, the same neighborhood that produced Hall of Famer Rod Carew and was the birthplace of Alex Rodriguez. Word got out after the *New York Times* dispatched reporter Sara Rimer, who wrote a series about Manny and his George Washington High School baseball team during his senior year.

DeLucca saw Ramírez for the first time in August of 1988 at the Parade Grounds at Brooklyn's Prospect Park. He had been sent to evaluate a first baseman on a Youth Service League team who was very talented, but rumored to have been living in a nearby crack house. DeLucca went to the park with Eddie Díaz, a former catcher who became a scout after his playing career. Díaz was a strong-looking guy who spoke Spanish and grew up in Washington Heights after leaving the Dominican Republic. He always tagged along with DeLucca, especially when he ventured into rougher parts of the borough or to scout Hispanic players, and he was particularly helpful on the day he came across Manny on the sandlot at Prospect Park.

When DeLucca arrived at the park, he found the prospect he came to evaluate had a pencil-thin physique, a drawn-out face, and rings around his eyes, confirming the scout's suspicions about the first baseman's connections to drugs. So as to not waste the trip, DeLucca began assessing the talent on the surrounding sandlots. That's when he laid eyes on Manny Ramírez in the batter's box.

Giordano would agree later, upon seeing Manny take batting practice, that he had tremendous bat speed. He commented that Manny swung just about the best bat he had ever seen. That's quite a superlative coming from the same guy who scouted Reggie Jackson and Cal Ripken Jr. This kid was quick, exact, and he was only fifteen! The hitting mechanics needed some adjusting, but that could easily be fixed with instruction. However, Manny's plate appearance that day in the park piqued DeLucca's interest enough that he sent his companion, Díaz, to meet him after he jogged in from center field. DeLucca instructed Díaz to write the boy's phone number and school on the back of a business card; after all, they wanted to have a way to get in touch with him again.

Díaz also grabbed some old batting gloves from the car—a pair he used when he played for one of Cleveland's minor-league affiliates—and presented them to Ramírez in the dugout as a token from their meeting. This gesture drew the attention of Mel Zitter, who ran the YSL program and looked after his players' interests when scouts became involved, and he confronted DeLucca afterward. There would be no scouts luring his kids to sign contracts for a worn set of gloves, and Zitter forbade him from getting close to the players. It was classic Zitter, but it was a trait DeLucca respected: he was the kids' only safety net protecting them from disingenuous scouts looking for bargain signings.

In Zitter's warning, he never told DeLucca that he couldn't try calling Ramírez. After a week, the scout referred to the number on the reverse side of the business card and waited for the boy to answer on the other end of the line. Only there would be no such luck: Manny didn't give him a working number. The Ramírez family didn't even have a phone in their apartment. Maybe the boy was bashful and gave Díaz arbitrary digits, saving himself from embarrassment. In any case, it wasn't an emergency. DeLucca and a handful of scouts from Cleveland and around the league were always there to watch Manny's every move anytime he set foot on a diamond over the course of the next four years.

Associate scouts like Díaz went to see the boy when DeLucca couldn't. DeLucca was responsible for evaluating every prospect from New York to New England, and Manny was always playing ball. Ramírez had five or six games per week, split between his high school and YSL teams, whose game settings were altogether different.

The Spanish-speaking community turned out for George Washington's contests, chanting and cheering from the first pitch through the final out. It reminded DeLucca of the vociferous crowds in Santo Domingo, who rallied for teams like the *Leones* and *Tigres* of the Dominican professional league. Manny was thirteen when he moved from Santo Domingo to New York, so he was familiar with the games' electric feel and all the chatter. It charged him up in the batter's box. He was a three-time All-City selection who hit .650 his senior year, swatting 14 home runs over twenty-two games, en route to being named the Public School Athletic League's (PSAL) Player of the Year.

All the commotion around the high school games would have been a distraction in the field for typical teenage sensations with major-league aspirations. For that reason, DeLucca speculates, Manny's high school manager had him play third base so he could talk to him through the game and keep him focused. The turf and dirt on the public schools' infields weren't exactly pristine, but the conditions didn't take away from Manny's performance. He routinely made clean picks and showed off a plus-arm from the hot corner.

"He really could have been a third baseman," DeLucca notes.

In fact, that's where the Mets worked him out when they evaluated him before the draft . . . but that's not where the Indians envisioned him. The club preferred him in the outfield. That's where DeLucca saw him most, patrolling center field for his YSL teams. He ranked

Manny as the top prospect in the region when he sent monthly reports to Mickey White.

George Lauzerique, the Indians' East Coast scout, praised Ramírez but cautioned Joe DeLucca about tabbing him as a top choice.

"I love this kid, but he ain't ever gonna be a first rounder," DeLucca remembers Lauzerique saying. George Lauzerique was from Cuba and had been in Manny's shoes before, having been drafted by the Kansas City Athletics after a promising career of his own at George Washington High School. Teams didn't roll the dice on Latin-American immigrant kids in the first round in those days, as the U.S. dollar was worth fourteen times more when converted to Dominican *pesos oros* at the time of Manny's MLB debut in 1993. Because Ramírez was in the country on a green card, who was to say that he wouldn't cash in on his signing bonus and return to his homeland to enjoy his fortune with friends and family? He was also going to be nineteen and would not finish high school. Was this kid worth the risk?

Mickey White certainly thought he was.

"There's a million reasons not to do something, and only one to do it," he says, looking back at the decision. "I believed Manny was the right guy. There are players out there who play because they are almost obsessive-compulsive about baseball. That's something that resonates clearly at that level of player. I'm still obsessed with baseball; not to the point that I don't eat or sleep, but the passion and curiosity that I have for the sport is still there. If you've got that in your heart and you see that in another player, there's a sentiment that resonates like a string being plucked."

Mickey White and John Hart went to the Big Apple to see Ramírez play again in person, as Cleveland had other viable options it needed to consider for its first selection of the draft. Danny O'Dowd had been lobbying for Aaron Sele, a 6-foot-3-inch right-hander who starred at Washington State University. The front office saw another potential choice in Allen Watson, a southpaw from the New York Institute of Technology in Long Island. John went to see Watson pitch at 10:30 one Sunday morning in Levittown and then trekked to Prospect Park to watch Ramírez. He saw Manny hit a long drive as soon as he got out of the car and started raving about his swing on the way to the field.

On the return flight back to Cleveland, Hart asked White what he thought about the players, and the scouting director was just as enamored with the kid from Santo Domingo and his sweet swing. Mickey was ready to sell him on his first pick.

"John, you know I'm from Pittsburgh. I told myself, if I ever had a chance to draft Roberto Clemente, this is the closest thing I've seen to him," White said. There was no disagreement from Hart. Now it was a matter of making an offer, drafting, and signing the kid.

The Indians had failed three times to get in touch with Ramírez to determine his willingness to sign, so DeLucca got a hold of Mel Zitter to act as an intermediary. There had been a time that DeLucca thought Zitter was acting as a bird dog for the Cubs, as that was the speculation around his YSL fields. Bird dogs referred players to teams' regional scouts and occasionally earned kickbacks when those prospects signed. Zitter got that reputation after some of his players (most notably Shawn Dunston and, later, Alex Arias) signed with Chicago. DeLucca would not feel comfortable talking to Manny if he was already being shuffled to the Cubs.

Zitter was receptive to the scout's concern and assured him that it was not the case. After quelling DeLucca's apprehensions, Zitter set up a date for the Indians to meet with Manny to conduct his signability.

The meeting place was a twenty-four-hour diner called George's near Prospect Park. Giordano went with DeLucca per their general manager's request. Zitter insisted on joining them, too, lest the team's representatives try to pull a quick one with his player. The three men chatted in a booth, waiting for Manny to arrive. DeLucca was relieved when he looked out the diner window and saw him hop off the bus across the street.

Manny sat down at the table and DeLucca could tell that he was shy. He ordered a bowl of soup, a hamburger, and a soda, which he scarfed down. The scout tried engaging him with questions about his parents and siblings, his school, his girlfriend, and if he really wanted to be a baseball player. Manny didn't look up from the table, nodding and responding with "uh-huhs" between bites. He looked over at Zitter for additional cues but slowly started to open up, especially after Giordano offered him another round of food. Manny first shook his head no, but Zitter flagged a waitress and ordered him a second helping anyway.

DeLucca interjected after Manny finished eating.

"Now look," he said, "You know why we're here. If we should draft you, would you play for the Cleveland Indians?"

Zitter let him answer.

"Yeah, I like the Indians," Ramírez said. Giordano later asked Zitter what it would take to sign Manny. He needed to give the management in Cleveland an estimate.

Zitter said it depended on what round they were thinking.

"We're talking the first round," Giordano said. DeLucca promised they would be fair to him. They weren't going to cheat him out of the money he was going to be due.

Zitter's jaw dropped as the scene unfolded: He was in disbelief, and it indicated to DeLucca that no other team had contacted him about making Manny their top priority. Only one other team, the Minnesota Twins, projected Manny's name to be called before the fifth round at the earliest.

Zitter had come prepared, armed with a list of signing bonuses awarded to the 1990 draft picks. His demands: The discussion for Manny's services started at $10,000 more than the Indians' first-round pick from the previous year, plus 10 percent. The Indians estimated that would bring the bonus to about $300,000, which was still an unheard-of sum for a mid-first-round high school pick. In comparison, Ken Griffey Jr. only got $160,000 from the Mariners for being the top pick in the '87 draft but wasn't anywhere near the record-setting $1.5 million the Yankees awarded Brien Taylor, whom they took with the No. 1 pick in 1991. Manny's money would be most comparable to the $275,000 that Larry "Chipper" Jones received when the Atlanta Braves drafted him out of Florida State as the first pick in 1990, and John Hart could have thrown in more cash if DeLucca needed it to sign his prospect.

DeLucca went out to the park to talk to Zitter at YSL's Sunday doubleheader. It was blistering hot for only the first week of June. As if the heat weren't enough to wear him out, Manny had worked out in front of the Mets for six hours the day before and had blisters on both hands. It didn't stop him from hitting eighteen balls out of the park during batting practice the next day; however, he was dragging by the second game, and it showed.

The Seattle Mariners' leading scout and the assistant to the general manager were on hand and saw a lackluster performance from Manny at the park, marked by a poor showing in the batter's box and an uncharacteristic lack of hustle. Nevertheless, their presence gave DeLucca a tinge of nervousness. Could the M's suddenly be interested in signing his top pick? Seattle was two slots ahead of Cleveland at No. 11. The Mariners' personnel caught up with Zitter along the foul line in right field after the game and chatted for about ten minutes, but when they passed DeLucca on the way to the parking lot, they wished him luck. DeLucca interpreted this to mean that the Mariners were not pursuing Ramírez after all.

The next day, the Indians selected Manny Ramírez with the 13th pick of the 1991 draft. Giordano flew out to New York and met DeLucca for the signing, which took place in the Ramírezes' apartment in Washington Heights. Zitter was there, too, and he collected a $10,000 check from the Indians to put toward his YSL programs.

When Giordano returned to Cleveland with the signed contract in tow, the congregation in the office let out a cheer. The Indians finally had their first-round pick.

* * *

The scouting department's successes in the 1991 draft didn't stop with the selection of Manny Ramírez. Cleveland went on to draft Florida Gators third baseman Herbert Perry with their second round pick, and LSU Tigers pitchers Chad Ogea and Paul Byrd heard their names called by the Indians in the third and fourth rounds. All three players were playing in the big leagues by 1995.

In all, the Chet Montgomery and Mickey White eras saw almost fifty players reach the major leagues.

"That's an aberration, in terms of numbers," White says. "If you have that many guys coming from your system at one snapshot, odds are it's a direct indication that you've done a good job scouting."

And it was a good reflection on Hank Peters for his staff's ability to complete one of its principal tasks in his final draft. Hank felt content

In only his second major league game in 1993, Manny Ramírez hits two home runs at Yankee Stadium. *AP Photo/Kevin Larkin.*

leaving the Indians with an arsenal of young talent, from which the organization could make call-ups to the majors in the coming seasons or swap as trade bait. He left Cleveland in a much better place than where they had been when he took the reins.

CHAPTER 8

A DAY WITH TY COBB

F. C. LANE

The public never tires of Ty Cobb and his marvelous exploits. He is the idol of the diamond, the one superplayer in the ranks. But the view of a national character in the limelight and in the privacy of his own home are essentially different things, hence the following sketch is offered as throwing new light on the complex character of the game's greatest player.

All night I had been riding through the heart of Dixie on a rheumatic old sleeper that groaned and bounded at every joint in the rusty rails. Indistinctly through the intervals of a broken sleep I recalled Sherman's famous march through Georgia and his celebrated remarks thereon. And the truth of those remarks was fairly jostled into my bones. Somewhat wayworn and threadbare in spirit, "early on a frosty mornin'" I dismounted at Augusta.

With one hand hastily inserted in my overcoat and the other on my grip I wended my way into the station and asked for a city directory. The attendant looked at me vaguely and remarked, in a far-off voice, that they had none. A friend, who was lounging near chewing tobacco with great industry, offered the suggestion that they might have one in the baggage-room.

In this receptacle of battered trunks I found two or three human beings, one of whom produced from beneath a crushing load of papers and nondescript refuse a moth-eaten directory.

"Ca," "Ci," my eye wandered down the "C's" till I stopped opposite a familiar name in the "Co.'s." "William Street?" I queried, "What car do I take to go to William Street?" The minion of Southern transportation gazed vacantly at me. "What part of William Street do you want to go to?" he asked. "I don't know," I replied. "The page is torn here, but I want to see Ty Cobb." Instantly there was a transformation in that inanimate posture. "Ty Cobb!" The baggageman straightened up and repeated the syllables after me with a world of respect. "Ty Cobb!" the listening assistants echoed. "We think a good deal of Ty Cobb down here," repeated the baggageman, and then he proceeded to tell me with the most painstaking exactness just how I should reach that home which is the most treasured spot in Augusta.

In due time no doubt from an Augusta standpoint a trolley car appeared in sight. I entered and told the dreamy-eyed conductor that I wished to alight at William Street. "William Street," he murmured vacantly, "that can't be on my route, I never heard of it."

"They told me in the baggage-room that this was the right line to take to reach Ty Cobb," I remonstrated.

"Ty Cobb!" said the conductor. "Oh, I know where he lives all right. Couldn't tell you the name of the street but I know the house. We go quite near it, you can see it from the car window. I will point it out to you when we get there."

It isn't the glare of publicity which shows a well-known personage in his proper light. It is rather the tiny rays that are thrown upon his character, the little things which indicate him as he is. And these two trivial experiences will show as clearly as anything else how Ty Cobb is esteemed among his neighbors.

A prophet is not without honor save in his own town, is often true of a ballplayer. Greenville doesn't exactly enthuse at the name of Joe Jackson. Carnegie, Penn., doesn't knock off work when Hans Wagner comes to town. The wheels keep right on moving at Meriden, Conn., when Ed Walsh and Jack Barry are away. But Augusta, Ga., has incorporated Ty Cobb in the city charter. His fame is her fame. His friends are her friends. And if perchance Ty Cobb has enemies, and so strong-minded an individual as he could scarcely help having enemies, they had best remain away from the genial Southern city on the Savannah river.

After climbing sundry hills and descending valleys equally numerous I was beginning to wonder if Ty Cobb had moved out of the state when the conductor whistled. Not being used to that kind of a signal I looked around and saw that he was motioning me to alight. "That's his house over there among the trees," he said and pulled the bell rope.

The Cobb home is a typical Southern mansion with a great broad veranda running about it, an easy display of room which lends an hospitable air to the mansion most in keeping with the character of its inmates. I didn't have time to ring the bell for Ty himself had the door open and was extending his hand in welcome while I was still mounting the steps. His huge car was throbbing and pulsating in the road beside the house all ready, I imagined, to take its owner on one of his many excursions into the hills. But Ty himself explained the situation by saying that he had just called off a hunting trip that minute. I trust that such was the case and that the courteous host was not inconvenienced in his plans by my unexpected visit.

Hero worship is quite as much a part of normal life as eating three meals a day. We all respect men who have accomplished things above the ordinary. There are men who have done great deeds who never allow that fact to be crowded into the background. Face to face they are distant still. But anyone who meets the greatest ballplayer who ever wore a uniform will see only a vivacious young American full of life and enthusiasm and good cheer, and they will never glean from his unaided conversation that he ever accomplished anything whatever.

There are swell-headed ballplayers, we regret to say, just as there are individuals suffering from that distressing malady in all walks of life. But Ty Cobb is not one of them. On the field he isn't overly popular, perhaps. There is an undercurrent of envy in human nature which

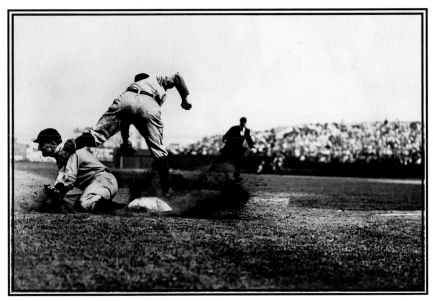

Ty Cobb stealing third base against the New York Highlanders. *By Charles M. Conlon via Wikimedia Commons.*

is sufficient to account for that. When Cobb is at bat or on the bases there is an all but uncontrollable impulse to show him up if possible. And Cobb is not an easy man to converse with in the heat of action. But although aggressive and audacious to the verge of desperation, he is not swell-headed. And off the field he is as democratic and easy to meet as anyone could wish.

But let us check up a day from the diary of the game's most famous player.

Ty gets up when he happens to feel like it. If he is going hunting the hour is the uncanny one of 3 A.M. or maybe earlier. If he hasn't anything particular in mind he gets up at 8 o'clock or later. Eating cuts no great figure in the Cobb establishment. Ty is so thoroughly a ballplayer, with the peculiarities of the craft, that he carries the summer habit of two meals a day right through the winter as well. If the fiery Ty needs only two meals when he is beating out lean bunts by lightning speed or playing a dazzling game in the field why should he need more in the season of rest?

An automobile is as Ty's right hand, and he has a good one, a high-power car that chugs with disgust at the hills of the neighborhood. When Ty wants to go anywhere he is always in a hurry and the car can't go any too fast to take him there. But the engine is already panting for action. We are off. Our first stop is at the Country Club. This fine building is set amid rolling hills, commanding a grand sweep of country and has, so it said, one of the best golf links in the South. "In the winter I am inclined to slight my game a little," says Ty, "for I am no enthusiast at golf. I like the game and see its advantages. It is good exercise, develops control over the muscles and benefits a player who has to bat for a living a good deal as batting practice does. The swing is different, the utensils used are different and you slug at a stationary ball instead of a moving one. And yet you have to hit right in either case and I believe playing golf helps a man's game at baseball."

Sometimes Ty tarries a while and follows the course around the golf links. Sometimes he stays only a few minutes to talk for a moment with some acquaintance—everyone knows him—and then speeds away to town. There, although Augusta is a thriving city of nearly sixty thousand inhabitants everyone knows him as well. People hail him from the sidewalks, crossing the streets, from other vehicles, everywhere. Ty's progress through town is a continuous revue. But there are certain vantage points where he is most likely to be found. One of these is the office of a local dentist. Here several choice spirits hang out and Ty is a frequent visitor. A particular hobby of the Georgian is dogs. While I was there he had a dog which was away at boarding school, being trained for etiquette, table manners or something of the kind. Cobb was interested in current events, still more so in baseball happenings, but most of all in that particular dog. One of the men in the office was training the dog, a sort of private tutor, and they had a long and animated discussion as to what should be done with this particular canine so as to make a good bird dog out of him at the earliest possible moment. My own knowledge of dogs, which extends just far enough to distinguish a bulldog from a greyhound, was not particularly illumined by the conversation. But that it was an unusually able and weighty one was well attested by the vigor with which Ty argued his point.

From this atmosphere of dogs and quail we proceeded to a music store. Next to four-footed beasts Cobb loves music. Well remembering a time last summer when he appeared late at a game in New York because he had to stop to hear the grand organ at Aeolian Hall, I was not surprised.

In this establishment Cobb had a friend as usual, a friend who was a composer. He played two of his own compositions, which Cobb criticised as frankly as he criticises an umpire's decisions.

"I have often wished I could become a composer," said Ty, in a retrospective mood as we whirled rapidly away, "but I don't suppose I have any talent along that line. Every man to his trade, and I guess mine is cut out for me. Baseball is a new game and you don't read in history of any men who became immortal by becoming great players. But any bid to anything out of the ordinary in my own case will be won on the diamond or not at all. And I know enough of fame on the diamond to realize that it lasts just as long as the ability is there to win it. I shall have my day like all the rest, and whatever I have done will be forgotten just as other records have been forgotten before. I always was ambitious, I guess. I used to think that if I were ever able to make a record on the diamond I would be satisfied. But people have been good enough to claim I have done no less and I am not satisfied."

"What will you do when you arc through with baseball?" I ventured.

"I have often asked myself that question and I have never gotten any answer which was quite satisfactory," said Ty, "but I suppose I will follow the line of least resistance and settle down to a quiet, uneventful life in the country, living all the year round much the same as I am living today."

"You might go into politics," I suggested. "No," he smiled and shook his head; "assuming I had any talent for the job I don't think I would like it. But I have no reason to suppose I have any talent along that line. And I can't write and I can't compose music, and what is there that I could do? Nothing that I know of save a humdrum life in the country. It looks rather welcome now for I get so much of the other kind, but I suppose I will get tired of it after I have lived it a while.

"I would like to travel, I think, when this war is over. They are making history now and we are living in the very pages that will afterward be written. Some day it will be worth while to walk over these great battlefields where the war is being fought out and I want to do that very thing. No, I haven't any decided notions in favor of either side. I believe the conflict was inevitable, according to the system followed by both parties in Europe. Some day, sooner or later, there was bound to be a crash, and it came rather sooner than most people expected.

"I went on the stage once, I didn't know but that it would be an interesting life. Of course, I didn't deceive myself into supposing I had any special ability as an actor, but I thought the life might be worth while. Maybe if a man could live without sleep and was made of cast iron it might be. But I found it hard, so hard that I want no more of it. I have passed up good offers since then, good from the financial standpoint, but I reasoned 'what is the use?' I am no hog. I am making money enough, money that with common sense will be all that I shall need. When I am through with the game, unless I experience some hard luck which I can't foresee now, I shall be independent and able to give my family a home and my children an education. The active season is enough for the whole year, for I don't get my money for nothing. There is a great deal expected and if I have one or two bad days I know how the grumbling grows.

A man has to deliver all the time and the more he is paid the more he has to deliver. I am pretty tired and stale when the season is over and if I risked my health through the winter for a few thousand dollars where would I get off in the long run? No, I settled all that for myself a long while ago. If I were a young ballplayer just breaking in and had a chance to earn money on the side I would take every dollar I could get.

But in my present circumstances I turn them all down. There is nothing in it. The man who tries to do too much doesn't do anything right."

Occasionally as we dashed through the streets Cobb would indicate a building. "I have an interest in that," he would say. "Most of your money is in real estate?" I asked. "Yes," he answered, "I like real estate and bank stock. I just invested a little money in some bank stocks a while ago. I think it is a good investment."

There is one room in the Cobb house which is always under lock and key. Ty carries the key. It is his room and its contents are never disturbed. A picture of that room would be worth while when he unlocked the door and escorted me across its forbidden portals. A mass of accumulated pictures, guns, trophies of the chase, a thousand and one knick-knacks lay scattered in profusion on the bureaus and the bookcases and the floor. On the shelf was a silver-hinged cigar box full of dollar cigars which a friend gave him for a present. "They're fine cigars," commented Ty, "though ten-centers are more in my line. What I brought you in for was to show you these books. I am a bug on Napoleon. Yes, that bottle up there is full of whiskey, moonshine whiskey, that a friend gave me. Patronize home products, you know. About Napoleon, I have all the books on his life that I ever heard of. I made a resolve to read two hours a day through the winter, but I don't always do it. So many things come up. But when I do read I find that I am most interested in Napoleon. He was a remarkable man. I never tire of digging up something about his life.

"That drawer is full of letters. Lots of people write to me, I don't know why. It bothers me more than any other one thing in the winter, those letters. I can't answer all of them, it would take too much time. I have thought of having a secretary. I guess I will have to get one if I ever catch up with my correspondence, but I have about given up hope. It bothers me, too, because I have the feeling that I am always neglecting someone."

Ty's parlor, drawing-room, or whatever he calls it, is a spacious apartment. It might well serve for an entire city flat. A spacious fireplace warmed the room and seemed to revive the reminiscent mood in which he fell when we seated ourselves before its welcome glow.

"I get into a lot of trouble by speaking too plainly," commenced Ty. "I have made enemies by it, I suppose, but my philosophy is brief. I claim that life is too short to be diplomatic. A man's friends won't mind what he says when they know his way, and those who are not his friends don't count. That's the way I look at it. I am glad this baseball war is all over. I guess everybody is, but I can see it will make trouble for the ballplayers. A good many people think the players have been having things too easy. Perhaps some of them have, but I have never seen a great deal of it in my experience. I know how hard I had to work to get a raise from $2,200 to $2,700 a year, and that was when I was leading the league in batting, too. Of course I got the big money later on, but I had been in the game some years and playing at top speed before I got it.

"The men in the Federal League were fine fellows so far as I saw them. Mr. Sinclair and Mr. Gilmore wanted me to join them and treated me royally. They made me some great offers; offers that I couldn't pass by without careful thought. But they had everything against them and from my own selfish reasons there was every consideration in the world which urged me to stay where I was. Other things being equal, as Walter Johnson says, a player gives his home club preference and the same thing goes for his league. I had made my record in the American League and preferred to stay there even though I could command a larger salary elsewhere.

"The Federal League offered me a tremendous salary, more than I am getting now; more, probably, than I shall ever get. But I couldn't see it. There were too many things which bound me to my own club.

"President Navin got worried, however. We have had our share of tilts, Navin and I, but I will say for him that he has used me well and I intend to do the same by him so far as I can. Still I always had sense enough to realize that it was purely a matter of business, that he would get his players to work for as little as possible and the players would try to get as much as possible. It is the old story of labor and capital, of supply and demand.

"He came to me one day and said, 'I would like to have you strike the ten-days clause out of my contract.' At that time the Federal League was making a great fight on that particular point and most of the organized club owners shook out the clause from their contracts, usually paying well for the privilege.

"I said to him, 'Why do you want the clause stricken out?'

"'I am beginning to think that maybe the contract isn't binding just as it is written with that clause in,' he answered.

"'Well,' I said, 'this is rather a late day to find it out. And if what you say is true, it means that I haven't had any claim on you since I have been working for you.'

"'That may be,' said Navin, 'but let's get together and fix it up now.'

"'Well,' I said, 'I don't see any rush about it. If you have been holding me over a trap door for nine years I ought to have the same privilege for a few days at least.'

"He didn't say any more at the time, but he came to me a few days later with much the same story. I suppose it was extremely cruel to keep him in suspense, but I couldn't resist the temptation.

Ty Cobb in 1910. *By Bain News Service via Wikimedia Commons.*

"But after he had mentioned the topic several times I said to him, 'It seems to me that you are pretty much concerned about this thing. I haven't asked you to take that clause out of my contract or to alter it in any way. I am still operating under the contract and have no complaint to make. I am satisfied but you don't seem to be. Now if that is the case and you want the contract altered it must be for some reason, and it must be worth something to you. Of course if you look at it in that light, it is my business to work for money, and I am open to reason—just what is your proposition?'

"I will tell you what his proposition was and I will let you see the contract. But I will ask you not to give out its contents."

And here Ty ran upstairs, two at a time as is his usual custom, and speedily returned with the document.

I will, of course, respect his wishes. The contents of his contract are as safe with me as they were on the original document. But for the curiosity of the public I will say that that contract called for a greater salary than was ever paid a ballplayer before, greater by a considerable margin than the highest salary, real or fictitious, ever ascribed to any other player.

As I scanned that contract I recalled the conversation I had had with Ban Johnson in the season when Ty Cobb was holding out for $15,000. Ban had showed more heat about the matter than is his wont, and just before I left he said, "If Cobb is waiting for the American League to pay him $15,000, he might just as well stay down in Georgia and pick cotton. The American League can afford to pay no such salaries and the American League will pay no such salaries."

But times change. In the American League Walter Johnson is reputed to draw a salary somewhat above $15,000 a year. So is Tris Speaker, while Collins' salary is supposed to equal that stupendous figure. But whether or not these famous stars draw the money they are reputed to draw Ty Cobb surmounts them all by a wide margin.

Recalling this episode Ty laughed. "I did stay out for a while before we came to terms," he said, "and I didn't find that the experience cost me money. I played in the neighborhood of twenty exhibition games and my share of the receipts was well over $2,000. The last game I played, if I remember, I took in over $400. So I lost nothing while the Detroit club was formulating the contract they were willing to give me. Of course I couldn't expect to keep up at this figure indefinitely, but I did pretty well as long as I worked at it."

Mrs. Ty Cobb, whom her husband calls "Charlie," is a woman of uncommon judgment and good sense. With a husband as high strung and temperamental as hers it is well that she is. A man of Cobb's quick, nervous disposition hasn't the most placid temperament in the world.

Cobb's two children partake of the family characteristics. The daughter Shirley, is Ty's special favorite, a quiet little maid of four years, with much of her mother's even disposition. Shirley always accompanies her father and he lets her steer the wheel of his big car for half minute intervals on a smooth road. The son, Ty Junior, is more high strung, more "like his old man," as Ty says.

Ty is particularly anxious lest his son grow up and become a mollycoddle. With his tutelage there is scant danger, as an incident in the young man's education (he is six years old) will show.

The youthful Ty got into an argument one day with another boy, and his visitor gave him every cause to feel resentment. Ty overheard the argument, and convinced that his son was not standing up for his rights, he called him aside. "Now," he said, "that boy may be older than you but he is no bigger. He has insulted you and if you don't go out and lick him I will lick you." Ty Junior, duly impressed by such logic, lived up to the reputation of his father in strenuous manner, and since that time there has never been any doubt of his wish or ability to insist on his rights.

Ty himself is of an aggressive, scrappy and hot-headed temperament. He has been in numerous scrimmages and no doubt will be in many more. But it is all a part of the day's work to him, a necessary adjunct of the strenuous life he leads and the various people good, bad and indifferent with whom he is unavoidably thrown in contact.

By way of illustrations two of Ty's historic scraps might be mentioned—one in which he assaulted a spectator in New York who had used abusive language, a scrap which resulted in the celebrated strike of the Detroit players and was indirectly instrumental in bringing about the Players' Fraternity.

Another was with a butcher in Detroit whom Ty thought had insulted Mrs. Cobb. This notable tilt for honor resulted in a sprained thumb and a sprained batting record for Ty.

But Cobb's scrappiness is really but an overflow of his nervous spirits. The man who is the greatest player the game has ever known must, perforce, be hung on steel wires, must fairly scintillate with nervous energy.

Ty is always in the forefront of progress and anxious to try out a new thing. A year ago he made a flight in an aeroplane, a flight that was little heralded at the time, to be sure, but one which he speaks about now with evident relish. "It was quite an experience," he said. "It happened at Pensacola, and a little Frenchman, the crack man of the place, took me up. I can't say that I would like the sport as a steady diet, but one voyage was interesting. I noticed that every once in a while the machine would seem to skid a bit, if I may use that word, though there wasn't anything to skid upon but air. It would jump and duck apparently a foot or two, and I commented on that fact when we alighted. 'A foot or two,' said the astonished aeronaut, 'when we struck those air pockets, we would drop sometimes fifteen or twenty feet. That's what seemed like a foot or two.'"

"Which one of your records do you prize most of all," I asked Cobb in an effort to turn his mind to baseball themes.

"Which one would you expect?" he asked.

"The time when you batted for .420." He shook his head.

"That was a great record," I argued, "they said no one would ever bat .400 again. "It's medium hard to hit .400," Ty conceded with a smile, "but I don't think most of that."

"The time you stole 96 bases," I suggested.

"It's not easy to steal 96 bases," admitted Ty. "You can't let the grass grow under your feet. A man has to get on base a good many times to steal 96. You can figure it out yourself. He has to bat well or get a lot of bases on balls or both, to reach first often enough to steal 96 bases, and then he has to have a number of other things break in his favor. If I had known at the beginning of the season that I was going to steal 96 bases I should have tried to take an extra spurt and made it an even hundred. I think I could have added four somewhere along the line, but, of course, I couldn't foresee the final score."

"The time you made 248 hits in a single season?" I asked. "No," he said.

"The time when you scored 147 runs?" "No."

"I won't keep you guessing any longer," he said. "The record that means most to me, and I will confess as much, is the record of leading the league nine years in succession. It has never been done before, and that is the hardest one of all from my way of thinking. A player getting everything in his favor and gaining a good start can burn things up for a season. But to hit at top speed for nine years running is a different thing again. I think if I am well that I have my eye on that little old ball for one year more, to make it an even ten. I think I can count on that, though there is no telling the opposition I may strike. After that I don't care so much. We all have our stint unconsciously perhaps. We all aim at a certain mark and when we hit it, if we do, we ought to be satisfied. That is my mark, my ambition to lead the league for ten successive seasons. And the thing I have done which means the most to me is that I have come within one of it already."

There was not the slightest trace of boastfulness in Ty's manner. There never is. He talked in a quiet, earnest way just as an amateur would talk of improving his game of golf. He was speaking of a record that has never been made, that if he succeeds in reaching, he will hold alone against the field. But that was part of his day's work, breaking records. That is what he is supposed to do. Yes, other players are paid to make hits and runs and put-outs, but Ty Cobb is the one player who is paid to make and break records—and he does it.

A tour of the yard to see the dogs (the smallest one was extremely affectionate. "The runt," said Ty, "he needs more attention than the others"); a visit to the barn to go through some of his things in a search for pictures, a casual word to Uncle Joe, who does the chores, and I was obliged to remind Ty that the train would soon be leaving.

"This is the way I live," said he, while we sped to the station. "A good many people come to see me. Those silver cups in the house were given to me by friends, that autograph picture of President Wilson was given me by the President before he was elected while on a trip to Augusta. But this is a typical day. Always glad to see my friends, you know to hunt or lounge around or play golf as the occasion requires. The winter is soon over and then another season's grind begins. Some of the players kick because I don't get much spring training. But I get my training right here. I am a little heavy now—weigh 192—but I don't take on weight very much. Pretty soon I will play golf every day more and more, and when I join the club I will be in prime shape. As it is, I get stale before the season is over. What would I get if I added a long training trip grind to my regular work? It isn't because I am lazy that I don't like training trips. It is because I know I wouldn't do my best work if I had to take them. President Navin understands, and he approves of my course, so why should anyone else care?

"Those northern cities are hard places to spend winter in," sympathized Ty, as I dismounted to the platform. "I stayed one year at Detroit. It was enough. If I had to live there I would get pneumonia. The sunny south is good enough for me, not that the Yankees aren't all right in the summer time. Couldn't get along without them, you know, and the war is a long time over down here." And he laughed. "No, you needn't hurry for the train. This isn't New York. Nobody hurries in Augusta. So long, I'll see you next summer," and he waved a good by from the platform as the train slowly pulled out from the station, bringing to a close a most enjoyable day with baseball's greatest player.

Editor's Note: Cobb batted .371 in 1916 , finishing second in the batting race to Tris Speaker's .386, ending his streak of nine consecutive batting titles. He then won three consecutive titles from 1917 to 1919, making it 12 batting championships in 13 seasons.

CHAPTER 9

FACING TED WILLIAMS

EDITED BY DAVE HELLER

BOB FELLER, Cleveland Indians, 1936–1941, 1945–1956:

When he first came up, he was a dead low-ball hitter, and you had to pitch him high and tight. . . . And after he was up there about a year, why he got to be fouling off the high fastball. He always was a better low-ball hitter throughout his career. You had to throw strikes to him. He would not swing at a ball unless it was over the plate—or he thought it was. He *seldom* ever took a called third strike that I know of.

If he got back too far [in the count], you'd try to throw a slider and catch the outside corner. . . . And you'd only throw the fastball inside to him so he couldn't get the barrel of the bat on the ball. He was a very good fastball hitter. Trying to throw a fastball by him was like trying to sneak a sunbeam past a rooster in the morning . . . very difficult. He might not hit it square, but he would certainly foul it back. He'd seldom miss. Most of your home run hitters are fastball hitters. He hit 10 home runs off me during his career, and his batting average against me was around .241 or .242, as far as I know.

* * *

Did our team use the Williams shift? Yes we did. [Actually,] we invented it, [though] it didn't affect him too much.[1] He'd hit those sinkers
over the infield—those line drive sinkers—or hit one out of the ballpark.

The Boudreau shift didn't really hurt him any, as far as his average
went. I only once saw him hit the ball to left field, which was a home
run in Cleveland in our old ballpark—Old League Park. We had the
shift on, the Williams shift, and he hit one purposely down the left
field line about 10 feet fair for an inside-the-park home run.[2]

Was he the toughest out [I ever faced]? No, I had a dozen fellows that
were tougher than Ted. A lot of left-hand hitters like Tommy Henrich
and Taft Wright, Stan Spence and Roy Cullenbine, who was a switch-hitter, Johnny Pesky, Nellie Fox, Rip Radcliff—they were all tougher than
Ted. DiMaggio hit me pretty good [as well]. He liked the ball away and
he had a stance where you couldn't pitch to him inside, because he would
have got hit if the ball got away from you. He would not move. He was
anchored right there at the plate and he wouldn't get out of the way of
the ball, so you had to be careful if you tried to pitch him inside, as you
were very apt to hit him. He was very close to the plate.

Ted hit as well as any hitter in any [era]. He was very good in the
clutch, like he was in the 1941 All-Star Game.[3] Williams went 4–4,

---

[1] The shift used against Ted was created by Indians manager Lou Boudreau after
game one of a doubleheader between Cleveland and Boston in July of 1946. It was
known as the "Boudreau" or "Williams" shift.

[2] On September 13, 1946, Williams hit an inside-the-park home run at Cleveland
against Red Embree in the top of the first inning in a 1–0 Boston victory. It was the
only inside-the-park home run of Williams's career.

[3] Williams hit a game-winning three-run home run off the NL's Claude Passeau in
the bottom of the ninth inning to give the AL a 7–5 win.

including a three-run home run off a blooper pitch thrown by Pittsburgh's Rip Sewell in the bottom of the eighth inning during the 1946 All-Star Game in Fenway.

[Ted] was a good friend of mine. We were very friendly socially away from the ballpark and even at the ballpark before the game. He spent quite a bit of time at my museum out in Iowa and helped me raise money to finish the museum—he and his son, John Henry.

Ted was three months older than me. He came up in 1939, and I came up in 1936,[4] though I didn't start pitching regularly until 1937. I got in a month and a week in 1936, and I became a regular pitcher in 1937, even though I missed a month because I slipped during a wet opening day game in Cleveland and tore up some ligaments in my elbow. I was out about a month in 1937, so I didn't pitch all that much. My first complete year of pitching, taking my turn every day, was 1938.

I have no idea why he didn't hit a home run off me before the war, but he just didn't do it; though he hit 10 home runs off me in my last ten years.

I only struck him out two or three times that I can remember. The first time was in Cleveland. It was just after the war or just before the war. He was very difficult to strike out. I'd throw him a changeup around his ankles and he'd pull it foul, and then I'd throw a slider around his fists—right around his belly button, around the belt buckle—and that was a good pitch for him. I don't know how many times he struck out in his career, but it couldn't have been many.[5]

---

[4] At the age of seventeen.

[5] Williams struck out 709 times in 9,791 plate appearances. He struck out over 50 times in a season just three times, and all of those occasions occurred prior to World War II, in three of his first four seasons in the majors.

Bob Feller gave up 10 of Ted Williams's 521 career home runs. *AP Photo.*

DiMaggio was tough to strike out, too, but Ted was a much better hitter and had more power, but he was not much of an outfielder when you got him out of Boston. He was a good outfielder in Fenway Park.

He had good, quick wrists and was a big, strong guy, and he had a big, heavy bat that he could handle very well, like a toothpick. He could hit to left field if he wanted to, but he rarely wanted to.

He was seldom called out on strikes. The umpires respected him. I never thought that the umpires gave him the benefit of the doubt. I never had any problem with that, not at all. I always thought the umpires were calling it right when Ted was up to bat while I was pitching. As far as I'm concerned, he didn't get any favorable calls. He had a good eye and very good hand-eye coordination, which is what made him so great.

MARTY KUTYNA, Kansas City Athletics, 1959–60, Washington Senators, 1961–62:

The first time I faced Ted Williams in 1960 was as a pinch-hitter on May 4. I came in relief with men on first and second and one out to face three left-handed hitters in the bottom of the eighth inning in Boston.

I got Vic Wertz on a fly ball. Then Ted Williams came up.[6] Harry Chiti was my catcher that day. He called for a slider, which I threw over the plate, and Ted had a good cut and fouled it off. Chiti came out to me and said, don't throw another one there, or he will hit it 400 feet. He told me to throw him inside. The next two pitches I did, and one of them was a strike, but umpire Nester Chylak called them [both] balls.

I took two steps forward and told the umpire they were strikes. The umpire came out to me and said next time you come toward me,

---

[6] With Boston trailing 5–3, Williams hit for Lou Clinton.

you'll be out of the game. The next two fastballs I threw were again inside and called balls. I walked Ted.

I shook my head and looked at Williams at first. Ted looked at me from first base and shouted, "They were all strikes, rookie!"

The next hitter was Marty Keough, and I struck him out to end the inning.

Ted Williams during spring training in 1958. *AP Photo.*

CHAPTER 10

THE ENGINEER: BOBBY COX

DAN SCHLOSSBERG

Connie Mack won 3,731 games. John McGraw brought his New York Giants home first 10 times and second 11 times. Casey Stengel won 10 pennants in 12 years with the Yankees, the same team Joe Torre brought to the postseason 12 straight times, with six pennants and four world championships.

But none of those managers finished in first place 14 years in a row.

Bobby Cox did that, guiding his Atlanta Braves to more consecutive regular season championships than anyone else in the history of professional sports. In fact, nobody else has come close.

No other club has even reached double digits. The Yankees of 1998–2006 rank a distant second in baseball with nine straight, while the Boston Celtics, Los Angeles Lakers, and Quebec Nordiques/Colorado Avalanche managed nine apiece in winter sports.

Only one other major league team has even reached double digits in consecutive playoff outings: the Yankees, with the generous boost of the wildcard, had 13 in a row from 1995 to 2007.

The Braves won because they had Bobby Cox, a director with the tenacity, talent, and fortitude of Steven Spielberg. When he talked, people listened (with the possible exception of the umpires).

It didn't matter whether the Braves played in the National League West, as they did when the streak started in 1991, or the National League East, which they dominated after realignment in 1994.

In every complete season from 1991 through 2005, Cox and the Braves finished first (a strike stopped the '94 campaign in August).

Like a master magician, Cox pulled rabbits out of the hat, sawed opposing teams in half, and managed to elevate himself, his coaches, and his players above the fray.

He won with fast teams, slow teams, speed teams, power teams, veteran teams, and even one injury-riddled team that required the influx and influence of 18 rookies. Ability mattered more than experience, with Andruw Jones and Rafael Furcal shining examples of players promoted to the varsity with résumés shorter than Sarah Palin's.

When Bobby banned music in the clubhouse, a rarity in baseball, he said he was doing it for several reasons: to create a businesslike atmosphere, to allow his players to concentrate on baseball, and to prevent arguments. There were no Latin quarters or neighborhood hangouts in his clubhouses. Everybody was treated equally.

Obviously, the system worked.

A third baseman who signed with the Dodgers but played for the Yankees, Cox found his calling after the Yankees gave him a chance to manage in the minors in 1971. Six years later, he served as first base coach of a world championship team in the Bronx and attracted the attention of Ted Turner.

Even though they had a few good men in Dale Murphy, free agent signee Gary Matthews, and future Hall of Famer Phil Niekro, the Bad

News Braves of 1978 wouldn't have won for Houdini. After four years of poor play and poor attendance, the impatient Turner canned Cox in favor of Joe Torre. The former Braves catcher immediately won a division title with the team he inherited.

Cox did not sit still. He crossed league lines again, landing in Toronto as manager of a Blue Jays team he would take to the 1985 American League Championship Series. Turner, who had second-guessed his initial decision to dump the dedicated young manager, then brought him back to Atlanta as *general* manager—and gave him ample money to rebuild the moribund minor league system.

With pitching his proclaimed priority, Cox acquired future Hall of Famers Tom Glavine via the amateur draft and John Smoltz via a trade for Doyle Alexander, Atlanta's top pitcher at the time.

Working in concert with scouting director Paul Snyder, Cox also scoured the amateur ranks for infielders Mark Lemke and Jeff Blauser, slugging outfielder David Justice, and left-handed pitcher Steve Avery—all key players in the worst-to-first team that started the 14-year title streak in 1991.

By then, Cox was managing the Braves again. He had returned to the dugout before the 1990 All-Star break at the behest of team president Stan Kasten, who vetoed Russ Nixon as field general while allowing Cox to keep both jobs for the rest of that season.

According to Terry McGuirk, who later became the team's chief executive officer, "Bobby might have showed his best talent as GM. He took an absolutely bankrupt situation and put together the talent, the coaches, the scouts, and the support system. But I don't think he was ever really comfortable in the role."

For the last half of the 1990 campaign, Cox kept his foot in the front office but his heart in the dugout. He even promoted an innovative but outspoken minor league pitching coach named Leo Mazzone.

Plagued by poor defense, the Braves didn't do any better for Bobby in 1990 than they did for him during his previous tenure. But that was before Kasten convinced John Schuerholz to leave the Kansas City Royals after the season.

The new GM rebuilt the infield, giving the young pitchers confidence that ground balls and pop-ups would become outs, and the Braves were on their way.

"My first taste of victory was the 1991 season," Cox said years later. "We had gone so bad for so many years. We improved our defense with Terry Pendleton, Sid Bream, and Rafael Belliard. Even though we were 10 games back at the All-Star break, we came back. It was the first time since 1982 our fans had anything to cheer about. They came out in droves. The city was completely energized. It was electric. It was the greatest experience."

The '91 Braves were the first team to reach the World Series just one season after posting the worst record in the major leagues. They won another pennant in '92 with a three-run rally in the last inning of the National League Championship Series. Then, after signing star pitcher Greg Maddux, they won 104 games, taking the 1993 NL West by one game over San Francisco in a title chase that went down to the final day. Two years later, Cox led the Braves to a world championship.

Having Maddux, Glavine, and Smoltz on the same staff helped; together with the Braves from 1993 to 2002, the threesome produced a staggering 648 victories—and would have won more if Smoltz had not spent three-and-a-half years as the closer.

"What made him a great manager was that he was so good at handling his players," Glavine said of Cox. "He was so good at getting the best and most out of his guys. He treated everybody with the utmost respect and made everybody understand that whether you were a superstar or the 25th man coming out of spring training, you were going to be at important piece of the puzzle. He made guys not only understand that but believe it.

"At one point people thought Bobby was digging his own grave by having three former managers (Jimy Williams, Don Baylor, and Pat Corrales) on the bench with him. But that's Bobby. He was comfortable in what he was doing. He wanted the best people around him to try and make the team as successful as he could. It turned out to be a pretty good formula."

In his book *Starting and Closing*, Smoltz also sang the praises of the pilot: "While Bobby helped lay the framework for our [14-year] run, he also deserves a ton of recognition for sustaining our run. You don't win any division for 14 years straight without finding ways to win games that you have no business winning, statistically speaking.

"Bobby's moves were always calculated, made with the intention of preserving a lead, preserving his athletes, or generating some offense when the run support well had run dry. He knew things the rest of us didn't know, saw things even the best in the game didn't see."

Thanks primarily to their future Hall of Famers, the 1998 Braves won 106 times, a franchise record, but Cox would add three more triple-digit seasons. The only previous pilot to post six 100-win seasons anywhere was Joe McCarthy, nicknamed "the push-button manager" because his Yankees seemed to win without much effort from the bench.

Cox worked hard, especially after the Braves lost Glavine and Maddux to free agency. Smoltz was actually the only player to share the entire 14-year run in uniform with Cox and Mazzone.

In 2005, the last year of the streak, the wily manager employed 18 rookies, with all but six making their major league debuts. Forced to fill in for injured regulars Chipper Jones and Johnny Estrada, plus ailing pitchers Tim Hudson, Mike Hampton, and John Thomson, Cox proved himself a master juggler. He still produced a 90-win season for the 14th time and finished first for the 15th straight time (counting his last year in Toronto but not counting the incomplete seasons of 1990 or 1994).

His teams won 2,504 games—fourth all-time among managers—in a 29-year career that stretched from 1978 to 2010. The Bobby Cox résumé included 15 division titles, five pennants, two knee replacements (perhaps from making so many trips to the mound), and a world championship—not to mention a record 158 ejections.

"He was thrown out more than any manager but that's because he took the game to heart and stood up for his guys," said Fredi Gonzalez, who succeeded Cox as manager of the Braves after the 2010 campaign.

"I grabbed him one night," said longtime Cox lieutenant Pat Corrales, a former manager himself. "I could see him starting to blow. So I grabbed him around the chest. He said, 'I'll fire you if you don't let me go.' I said, 'Then you're going to have to fire me because I'm not letting go.' I just hung on until I realized he wasn't going to do anything."

Another Cox coach, Ned Yost, told writer Jayson Stark that Cox had two personas. "He's the nicest guy in the world," he said. "Just don't get him mad at you. If he ever gets mad, he turns into Mike Tyson. He doesn't care who you are or what you are."

After Cox sprayed Jerry Crawford with tobacco juice during an argument, he always made it a point to take whatever he was chewing out of his mouth before going out to argue. "It just happened," said

Crawford, "and he was upset about it and wanted to make sure it didn't happen again."

Although he argued with umpires often, Cox was a player's manager whose rules were simple: show up on time and play hard. It was not uncommon for stars of other teams to express a desire to play for him.

Because of rapid changes in baseball economics, Cox was handed a new deck of cards every spring. But he always managed to make the most of what he had. On the rare occasions when he found a joker in the deck, Cox cut ties quickly.

Players like Deion Sanders, Kenny Lofton, John Rocker, and Bret Boone did not fit the Cox formula of a businesslike clubhouse devoid of such distractions as the raucous rock music that permeates and often divides other locker rooms. Bobby Cox teams did not have cliques or controversies other than the usual moaning and groaning from players perplexed by his penchant for platooning.

Cox protected his players, never complaining about them publicly, and took the blame himself when things went badly.

When they did, however, even star players didn't escape the manager's scrutiny. In 1998, Cox replaced Andruw Jones in the middle of an inning after the star centerfielder made a halfhearted effort to catch a fly ball. The lesson, though embarrassing, was learned: Jones won 10 consecutive Gold Gloves and earned comparisons to Willie Mays for his spectacular defensive play.

"The greatest compliment I could ever give a manager is to say I would have loved playing for him," said Hall of Fame pitcher Don Sutton of Cox. "As much as any manager I've been around, Bobby had loyalty from his players and coaches—a commitment from every one of them to do the right thing. That's something very few managers can say."

The first man named Manager of the Year in both leagues, Cox won the official award from the Baseball Writers Association of America four times. When the *Sporting News* polled his peers, however, Cox won the honor six times—twice as often as anyone else.

His best performance might have come in 2004, when his Braves won 96 games—topping the division by 10 games—after losing Greg Maddux, Gary Sheffield, Javy Lopez, and Vinny Castilla to free agency and Marcus Giles and Horacio Ramirez to injury.

Before both he and Cox were inducted into the Baseball Hall of Fame in 2014, Tony La Russa recalled his initial impression of Bobby.

"When I was with the White Sox and Jim Leyland was one of my coaches, we used to face Billy Martin, Sparky Anderson, Earl Weaver, and Gene Mauch," he said. "But all of a sudden this new guy goes to Toronto and after a series or two, we looked at each other and said, 'Hey, this guy's pretty good.' It turned out to be Bobby Cox.

"In 1996, when I got to the National League for the first time, the Braves were the world champions and Bobby was on that incredible run of division titles. I had known him during the winter—he's a terrific guy, sociable and fun—and I was looking forward to saying hello when we went to play his team. I saw him standing at first base. I was expecting a big hug and a nice conversation. He waved but that was it.

"He made it real clear that it was his team against your team and there was a score. I've always felt that Bobby was the very best at sending the message that said, 'If I see you this winter or in the restaurant after a game, I'll say hello and ask how your family is and wish you well since you're in a different division.' But playing against him, he and his team competed and they were going to beat you."

Jeff Torborg, who managed three different teams against Cox, agreed. "What I liked about Bobby was that he was so consistent," said Torborg, a former catcher who served as pilot of the Mets, Expos, and Marlins. "No show, down to earth, very genuine.

"That streak (of 14 titles) was unbelievable. He called me one time, asking about somebody in the administrative level, and the next thing you know, we're trying to make a trade. But he wasn't going to give up one of those young pitchers if his life depended on it. Avery was the guy we thought might be available. No chance. When you think about what he did—how he set it up, then went down to the field to make it work—his career was just incredible."

Bobby Cox did more than push buttons; he had a gift for meshing many different personalities and persuading them to maximize their potential.

According to John Schuerholz, who succeeded Cox as general manager and retained the position throughout the 14-year run, "Bobby had such great talent: his instincts for dealing with people, his ability to communicate in his own inimitable fashion, plus the respect he has for the game and the players who play it at the highest of all levels. It's so clear and obvious to them that they gave back to him in double or triple measure the same amount of respect. He held them in such high esteem, and expected so much of them. That was the attitude and professionalism he brought to the ballpark every day.

"I don't think anyone will ever win 14 consecutive titles again. I had the great pleasure of working side by side with him to marshal our plan and keep it in place. It's a remarkable feat no one will see in our sport or any other sport in our lifetime."

Atlanta Braves manager Bobby Cox (right) in the dugout with pitching coach Leo Mazzone in 2003. *AP Photo: Gregory Smith.*

CHAPTER 11

THE METHUSELAH
OF THE MOUND

LEW FREEDMAN

The man who may have been the greatest pitcher in baseball history watched in dismay as the world passed him by. Then, in an instant, Satchel Paige went from being overlooked to grandly exposed in the baseball fraternity.

For years Paige had blown away hitters with his mix of blurring fastballs and complicated off-speed stuff featuring a "hesitation" pitch. He engaged in stunts such as waving his fielders in and striking out the side and bragged about his throwing prowess in a way that would not otherwise become part of the athletic landscape until such broad personalities as Muhammad Ali and Joe Namath ascended in the 1960s.

He was baseball's best-kept secret, a pitcher on par with Dizzy Dean and Bob Feller—and those finest Major League mound stars said so, too—yet he operated in the shadows, where there was little media attention.

A showman deluxe, the gangly Paige befuddled hitters wherever he traveled—and boy did he travel—in the Negro Leagues, in foreign countries, and for barnstorming exhibitions. No one could hit his stuff with any consistency. He jumped teams and contracts at will because he was bigger than the boundaries set by his leagues and his clubs, chasing the dollar wherever it was offered. Sometimes he had large wads of cash in his pockets, and that's why he took to carrying a handgun.

Paige knew how good he was, and he wasn't shy about telling anyone willing to listen. Mostly those were black Americans who turned out in droves when his name appeared on a marquee. They were also sportswriters representing newspapers like the *Chicago Defender* and *Pittsburgh Courier,* whose audiences were black readers.

More than once Paige was told that if he were only white he would be signed by a Major League club in a second. But he knew that without being told. He knew that the work he did for the Pittsburgh Crawfords, the Kansas City Monarchs, and other black teams, or the throwing he did in Mexico, the Dominican Republic, or in other Latin American nations where he was welcome, was more than just good enough. Paige was endowed with a rubbery right arm of extraordinary endurance, a fastball of super speed, and a confidence level that enabled him to master every situation on the ball field he faced, even if he was facing a Josh Gibson or Buck Leonard, two of the most feared Negro Leagues hitters of the day.

It was the rest of American society that occasionally kept Paige off balance, though few prominent African Americans coped with the hatred and discrimination that pervaded the country in the 1930s, 1940s, and beyond as well as he did. No one ever invented a machine that could measure motivation, but if there was a graph chart to accompany such results, Paige's hunger and desire to prove himself would have been over the top.

It was not skill alone that lifted Paige to the top of his game. He was a star in personality, as well. Some people are born with charisma as well as talent, and Paige was a man who innately understood how to please an audience. Pitching skill is one thing. A player must possess enough talent to overwhelm big-league hitters. But putting on a show at the same time, ah, that was something special—something that only a few could master. Paige was the king of the hill when it came to combining outstanding performance, crowd-pleasing chatter, and colorful antics.

There was part of Paige that was definitely a guy who enjoyed hamming it up, but he never lost sight of his primary goal—to set the batter down and chalk up an out. Paige could be playful and purposeful simultaneously, but whether it was couched in such a way that the flavor of the moment was remembered by onlookers or not, Paige never was anything but serious about his pitching.

Paige was immensely proud and quite aware that his gift on the mound was what set him apart from others. He deeply resented being stuck on the outside looking in at the National Pastime, but he rarely showed his frustration in either deed or words except when tested on the field. He said a lot, but when it came time to get the important message across, he always let his arm do the real talking.

"Satchel's the greatest pitcher ever lived," said Ted "Double Duty" Radcliffe, both a teammate and opponent of Paige's.[1]

No one—not even Paige—knew how many games he won as he crisscrossed the country, switched leagues, and swapped teams. He sometimes made cameo appearances lasting three innings. The show was the thing in exhibitions. Fans wanted to go away saying they had seen the great Satchel Paige work his wizardry.

Paige grew up in Mobile, Alabama, not one of the forward-thinking American communities on race during the first two decades of the twentieth century. However, Mobile was a cradle of great baseball stars, including future Hall of Famers Hank Aaron and Billy Williams.

Paige's given name was Leroy, and he was one of John and Lula Page's (the spelling of the last name changed later) eleven children. Growing up, Paige's favorite hobby besides baseball was fishing, a passion he indulged the rest of his life. During his youth he earned his nickname of "Satchel" through work carrying suitcases for arriving passengers at the local train station. He developed a gizmo that enabled him to tote more than one at a time, earning the lifetime sobriquet. However, Paige also got into trouble as a teen and was sent to the Alabama Reform School for Juvenile Negro Lawbreakers for five years, and it was there he truly learned the art of pitching. His motion was perfected partially by repetitive rock throwing. Eventually, he made his professional debut, being paid $50 a month, for the Chattanooga Lookouts in 1926.

Paige was brilliant at getting what he wanted: a larger paycheck, the right to drive his own Cadillac to games rather than riding the bus, or being the headliner when the most important games were played. Paige was always stung that he was not wanted in the majors because he was black. Much like basketball player Darryl Dawkins, who later named his spectacular slam dunk, Paige had a variety of names for the repertoire of his pitches, changing them on a whim. Some were crisper than others, but among the titles applied were "bat dodger," "hurry up ball," "wobbly ball," "nothin' ball," and "midnight creeper." Cool Papa Bell, another of the brilliant Negro Leagues players of Paige's vintage, said, "Bob Gibson was fast, but Satchel was faster than all of them."[2]

If Paige was ever the least bit timid on the mound, he had out-grown any hint of trepidation by the time he was pitching for pay. He learned early that his best pitches were too much to handle for even the best hitters. When you strike out 17 opponents in a game, as Paige was doing in his teens, it becomes apparent early that you can fool most of the hitters most of the time. Usually, a leveling-out process follows when even the best pitchers can't dominate. But things never evened out for Paige. He never found a league he couldn't dominate.

"All I know for sure," Paige said in his folksy way, "is that there's a fellow at that plate with a big stick in his hand. It's him and me and maybe he'll hurt me. But if he does, he's got to hit that fastball."[3] Those fellas carrying big sticks rarely did.

Paige was a mythmaker. In an era when little was documented and often only second-hand by newspapermen who were not present at the event, he could spin his skills any way he wanted. There was no Inter-net, no TV, and no radio of Paige's games. The eyewitnesses shrunk back into their homes when a game ended. Paige was free to embellish and he was a marvelous storyteller. The basic facts of the matter might be authentic in terms of wins and losses or number of strikeouts, but Paige had a talent for telling a tale breathlessly, building drama. Satch's version might be a life-and-death account, such as pitching for Presi-dente Rafael Trujillo, supposedly at gunpoint after spending a night in jail in the Dominican Republic. Paige could charm any listener, and his feats were impressive enough to support any backstory.

The American South was often seen as divided from and separate from the North during the early years of the twentieth century, as it had been during the Civil War. It remained backward on race relations with full-scale discrimination and Jim Crow laws in effect to restrict Afri-can Americans. There were "colored" and "white" drinking fountains in public places, segregated seating at movie theaters and ballparks. There were lynchings of blacks across the region for no better reason than a young African American male looking the wrong way at a white woman.

Daily doings and achievements by blacks were ignored—beyond the boundaries of the South. It was as if newspapers and magazines considered the minority population of the country to be invisible. That is one reason why descriptions of Negro Leagues baseball stars often referred to them as playing "in the shadows." It was as if whites and blacks lived in parallel universes.

The first true crossover American sports superstar was heavyweight champion Joe Louis. He was followed by Olympic sprinter Jesse Owens, whose multiple gold medals earned in the 1936 Summer Games in Berlin seemed a personal insult to German dictator Adolf Hitler. Jackie Robinson was next in line as the third athlete whose accomplishments earned fans of all colors and ethnic backgrounds.

Paige was an athletic god in the black community but for much of his career was known as a superior baseball player only by a sliver of the sport's constituency. Mainstream Americans did not follow Negro Leagues baseball. However, those who did not reside in Major League cities were the beneficiaries of traveling All-Star teams playing exhibitions in the offseason, usually in the early fall after the World Series.

Dizzy Dean, the St. Louis Cardinals' brash and brassy hurler who won 30 games in 1934 for the World Series champs, was a pioneer at pulling together postseason, pieced-together barnstorming clubs that often toured with and played against Satchel Paige–led all-black ensembles. Across the great divide of segregation these types of encounters showed Paige and his teammates that they were just as good as the white players. It provided empirical evidence otherwise unattainable.

Dean and Paige were quite the pair. They both threw fast; they both had disputes over their dates of birth; and they both liked to do nothing more in the world than talk a good game. They teased each other, entertained the public with one-liners, and became great friends. Dean was as much cornpone as Webster's in his speech, especially when the Arkansas boy tried to please his constituency. But he was never condescending to Paige, and he was always laudatory on the radio when he broadcast games and in the newspapers where he penned a column. Whether Dean could spell well or not was unknown, but his editors apparently felt attention to detail was not necessary when he wrote.

"I know whose the best pitcher I ever see and it's old Satchel Page [sic], the big, lanky colored boy," Dean wrote. "Say, old Diz is pretty fast back in 1933 and 1934, and you know my fastball looks like a change of pace alongside that little pistol bullet old Satchel shoots up to the plate. It's too bad those colored boys don't play in the big leagues because they sure got some great players." Dean added, "If old Satchel and I played together we'd clinch the pennant mathematically by the Fourth of July and go fishin' until the World Series. Between us we'd win 60 games."[4]

In later years, after Dean's Hall of Fame career was shortened by injuries, Paige and Cleveland Indians star Bob Feller engaged in similar touring showdowns and also gained mutual respect for each other. Paige was older and in theory on the downside of his career. It was the 1940s, not the 1930s prime of Dean. Yet Paige and Feller had their own road show. These barnstorming adventures were all about money, and nothing spoke louder to Paige than the color green. However, it was also important to him that he show well. It wouldn't do at all to come off as inferior to his white counterparts, even if Paige was believed to already be in his forties. Feller and Paige were also well aware that many of the baseball fans who would attend their events were curious about the black-versus-white aspects of the contests. Were blacks just as good at baseball as whites?

"The whole trip was because of racial rivalry," Feller said of a 1946 tour.[5]

With each star pitcher serving as captain of a racially divided team, the two groups of All-Stars toured the hinterlands where only minor league ball was regularly played. Stops included visits to Pennsylvania, Ohio, Missouri, Colorado, and California, and there were more than 250,000 paying customers. They did it again in 1947. Feller was not generous in his assessment of the African American talent, which his team bested regularly in 1946. "Maybe Paige when he was young," Feller said, indicating he was the only one among the opposition that was Major League–ready.[6] Much later Feller added to his impressions of Paige, saying he had "perfect control" and "could spot a hitter's weaknesses very quickly, quicker than anyone I ever knew."[7]

Although he rarely admitted his deepest true feelings, Paige did believe that if and when the white man opened to black players, his would be the first name called. Many times over the years he had heard the patronizing and infuriating phrase "If only you were white" about the likelihood of a big-league contract being offered. It was a shock to Paige when Branch Rickey and the Brooklyn Dodgers announced the signing of Jackie Robinson as the first twentieth-century African American player.

Paige believed he was going to be the chosen one, if there ever was a chosen one. To many, Paige was too old. One of the great mysteries of his life was the pitcher's actual age. Many theories abounded, and Paige played along with them when outsiders sought to trace his Mobile,

Alabama, birth to a specific date. Paige had also attained a certain stature in the sport. To some baseball fans his was the only name known in Negro Leagues ball. He was not going to be a man to kowtow to any elements of discrimination if he integrated the sport, and perhaps white owners feared that he was too much his own man.

Famously, when Rickey signed the much younger Robinson he asked him to turn the other cheek to the firestorm of discrimination coming. Paige did not have the makeup to cope with an order not to fight back as Robinson adjusted to in his first years. Paige disarmed some discrimination with cleverness and humor, but he was a very different kind of person than Robinson. Robinson was more disciplined and was married. Paige was a free-wheeling guy and a playboy at various times of his life.

Robinson made his Major League debut for Brooklyn in 1947. The Dodgers were in the forefront of integration. They were signing other African American ball players, too, like Roy Campanella, Don Newcombe, and Dan Bankhead. Bankhead became the first African American to pitch in a Major League game on August 26, 1947, when he hurled 3.1 innings for the Dodgers against the Pittsburgh Pirates.

Once Robinson jump-started the integration of the majors and others had started to follow, Paige believed his ship had sailed; the last opportunity for him to appear in the white majors was gone. *How about that*, he probably thought. The majors were looking for black talent and they didn't even know his phone number. They were dismissing him because he was too old. A certain amount of intimidation might also have played a part in teams ignoring Paige. He was set in his ways, and the reputation that preceded him was of a player who didn't work hard, who had a general disdain for the clock and keeping appointments (such as clubhouse arrival times).

However, Americans at large had caught a glimpse of this enigmatic figure some years earlier. In an unprecedented divergence from its usual journalistic practices, *Life* magazine ran a spread on Satchel Paige, a "negro" baseball player locked out of the majors because of his skin color, in June of 1941. In twenty-first century America, it is difficult to get across how significant *Life* magazine coverage was at that time. It was the official barometer of American life. It was the most important magazine in the nation. If *Life* magazine wrote about you and displayed photographs of you, that meant you really were somebody.

Paige was a sportswriter's dream. All he had to do was act his usual self and the writer would go away smitten by this genius of the mound who could tell tales like Mark Twain. And Paige knew exactly what he was doing. "The sportswriters loved me acting the big shot and living it up like that," Paige wrote later in life. "They started talking about me like I wasn't even a real guy. I was something out of a book."[8]

Early in his pitching career Paige realized there was no percentage in hurrying to the mound. He might strut off of it, but when he entered a game, Paige was in no rush. He recognized that until he threw the first pitch no action would transpire, so he maintained control of the pace. Paige also had a very noisy stomach that often gave him indigestion and was known to sip Pepto-Bismol or equivalents while on the mound. That was all backdrop to his legendary list of rules for smart living that became part of the Paige legend.

Entitled "Time Ain't Gonna Mess With Me" by *Collier's* magazine and later referred to generally as "Satchel Paige's Rules For Staying Young" by a variety of publications and in books, Paige listed:

1. Avoid fried meats which angry up the blood.
2. If your stomach disputes you, lie down and think cool thoughts.

3. Keep the juices flowing by jangling around gently as you move.

4. Go very light on the vices, such as carrying on in society. The social ramble ain't restful.

5. Avoid running at all times.

6. Don't look back. Something might be gaining on you.[9]

Some people probably remember portions of Paige's advice better than the man who had offered it. It was typical Paige. His comments were part sincere, yet offered with a wink given that he rambled as much socially as anyone in the sport. The "Don't look back" comment was the most enduring.

In 1948, it was getting more difficult for Paige to look forward. He saw a new world opening in baseball, and he wasn't part of it. Suddenly, Major League teams (at least some of them) were looking for talented African American players, and they weren't looking at him. In 1946, Paige had sent new Cleveland Indians owner Bill Veeck a telegram asking when he was going to be summoned to Cleveland. He was not hired at the time, but Veeck wrote him back a note that was hopeful in content, implying that patience was going to be needed.

The Dodgers were the most progressive team, almost seeming to be cornering the market on black talent. But the Boston Braves were showing signs of aggressiveness, as were the New York Giants. The American League was slower to integrate, but Veeck had made Larry Doby the first African American player in the AL only months after Jackie Robinson joined the Dodgers.

Veeck may well have once at least mentally committed to stocking a Major League club with black talent, but the 1948 Indians were not the early 1940s Philadelphia Phillies. This was a club on the verge of capturing a pennant, perhaps capable of reaching its first World

LEROY "Satchell" PAIGE

1949 Bowman baseball card of Satchel Paige. *By Bowman Gum via Wikimedia Commons.*

Series in nearly three decades. Yet by July Veeck was not completely convinced the Indians could go all of the way. He felt the squad needed some bullpen help.

The energetic owner was quite aware of Paige's skills, but he wondered if he had enough left in his arsenal to play big-league ball in 1948.

Like almost everyone else, Veeck was not sure how old Paige really was. It eventually came to light (after some light-hearted shenanigans by both Veeck and Paige) that Paige was born on July 7, 1906. That made him forty-two years old, not an age that appealed to any team looking for young prospects. But that wasn't what Veeck was looking for anyway. He was in the market for immediate help to give manager Lou Boudreau more options in the bullpen.

Veeck was friendly with Abe Saperstein, the creator and longtime owner of the Harlem Globetrotters. Saperstein and Veeck had both been based in Chicago for years. No one knew the African American sports scene better than Saperstein, and Veeck asked him to scout for potential fresh young black talent. A couple of African American players had been signed by the Indians organization, but they were only minor leaguers.

In 1948, Veeck approached Saperstein again and asked if he could arrange a tryout for Paige with the Indians. Veeck ran his brainstorm past Hank Greenberg, who had settled into the front office after his aborted fling in the field during spring training. Veeck was also aware that his own pitcher Bob Feller and Paige had developed a good rapport from their barnstorming experiences. Manager Lou Boudreau was not consulted in advance, but asked by Veeck to come to the ballpark to watch a pitching prospect throw.

"What could I do?" Boudreau said. "Veeck was the boss. I said I'd be there in an hour. It was then I met Satchel Paige for the first time. I told Satch to loosen up, to run or whatever, and let me know when he was ready. He stuck out his hand, jiggled it, then said, 'Mr. Lou,' which is what he always called me, 'I'm ready. I pitch with my arm, not my legs.'"[10]

Initially Boudreau did not respond warmly to the idea of the ancient (in his mind) pitcher becoming an Indian. Boudreau said he played catch with Paige for perhaps ten minutes while other witnesses on the scene, Veeck, Greenberg, Saperstein, and *Cleveland Plain Dealer* sportswriter Gordon Cobbledick watched in silence. Paige may have been old by baseball standards, but he also had a point to prove. To demonstrate that he was throwing as efficiently as ever, he gave Boudreau a handkerchief that was folded up into small squares and asked him to put it on the plate in any position at all.

"First I put it on the inside corner," Boudreau said. "He wound up and threw ten pitches—fastballs and sliders, all with something on them—and nine of them were right over the handkerchief. He told me to move the handkerchief to the other side of the plate and he threw ten more pitches the same as before. His fastball had a hop to it and his slider was tremendous. Seven or eight of his pitches were right over the handkerchief and those that missed didn't miss by much."[11]

The point was made that Paige had remarkable control. Of course, no one was in the batter's box, and pitching against live hitters was much different. It was Veeck who insisted that Boudreau take a turn in the box. After all, he was one of the best hitters in the American League. Boudreau said he struck a few line drives but saw enough to know that Paige still had the goods. Joking about Paige's true age began immediately upon his signing, Veeck told the reporters Paige was forty-two. Paige said he was "only about thirty-nine." Boudreau said he thought Paige might be closer to forty-nine or fifty. Boudreau saw value in Paige as a reliever and spot starter to mix into the pitching rotation.[12]

Although there was no such thing as a media storm to match the hurricanes of the 2000s, within the context of the times, the Indians signing Paige was big news.

The *Sporting News* offended both Veeck and Paige with its high-and-mighty reaction that bordered on the hysterical. The weekly

Sporting News was the Bible of baseball, and it was more conservative than extreme right politicians. Owner J. G. Taylor Spink authored an editorial, accusing Veeck of making a travesty of the game by inking Paige. "If Paige were white he would not have drawn a second thought from Veeck," Taylor wrote. "To bring in a pitching 'rookie' of Paige's age casts a reflection of the entire scheme of operations in the major leagues. To sign a hurler of Paige's age is to demean the standards of baseball in the big circuits."[13]

It was not unusual for someone to accuse Veeck of trying out a gag for publicity value. He was more proud than chastised most of the time when such a thing occurred. However, Veeck had too much respect for the black ballplayers who had been marginalized to trifle with their feelings. He knew Paige could still play. Veeck, who always called Paige Leroy, his real first name, and Paige became close friends, and as it became apparent that Paige was a valuable addition to the Indians, the owner sent messages to Taylor tweaking him about the newcomer's success and even suggesting Paige should be considered for rookie of the year honors.

The Paige accuracy and ball placement with the handkerchief was a neat trick, and Boudreau said, "Now I can believe some of the tall stories they tell about his pitching."[14]

Indeed, for Paige the handkerchief ploy was somewhat routine.

"I don't pitch for home plate," he said later. "I stick a small matchbox or a tiny piece of cigarette paper in front of the catcher instead," Paige said. "I figure if I can throw over a small target like a matchbox I sure can get it over a great big plate."[15]

Paige pitching in relief for the Cleveland Indians at Yankee Stadium in 1948. *AP Photo/Matty Zimmerman.*

NOTES

1. Holway, John, *Josh And Satch: The Life And Times Of Josh Gibson And Satchel Paige* (Westport, Connecticut, Meckler Publishing, 1991), p. xii.
2. Ibid., p. 11–12.
3. Tye, Larry, *Satchel: The Life And Times of an American Legend* (New York, Random House, 2009), p. 42.

4. Ibid., p. 95.

5. Ibid., p. 172.

6. Ibid., p. 173.

7. Ibid., p. 174.

8. Ribowsky, Mark, *Don't Look Back: Satchel Paige in the Shadows of Baseball* (New York, Simon & Schuster, 1994), p. 191.

9. Donovan, Richard, *Time Ain't Gonna Mess With Me*, Collier's Magazine, June 13, 1953.

10. Boudreau, Lou, and Schneider, Russell, *Lou Boudreau: Covering All the Bases* (Champaign, Illinois, Sagamore Publishing, 1993). p. 112.

11. Ibid., p. 112–113.

12. Ibid., p. 113.

13. Ibid., p. 111–112.

14. Dickson, Paul, *Bill Veeck: Baseball's Greatest Maverick* (New York, Walker & Company, 2012), p. 145.

15. Lebovitz, Hal, *Satchel Paige's Own Story*, (Westport, Connecticut, Meckler Publishing, 1948/1993), p. 64.

CHAPTER 12

THE GAME THAT
COST A PENNANT

CHRISTY MATHEWSON

The Championship of the National League was Decided in 1908 in One Game between the Giants and Cubs—Few Fans Know that it Was Mr. Brush who Induced the Disgruntled New York Players to Meet Chicago— This is the "Inside" Story of the Famous Game, Including "Fred" Merkle's Part in the Series of Events which Led up to it.

The New York Giants and the Chicago Cubs played a game at the Polo Grounds on October 8, 1908, which decided the championship of the National League in one afternoon, which was responsible for the deaths of two spectators, who fell from the elevated railroad structure overlooking the grounds, which made Fred Merkle famous for not touching second, which caused lifelong friends to become bitter enemies, and which, altogether, was the most dramatic and important contest in the history of baseball. It stands out from every-day events like the battle of Waterloo and the assassination of President Lincoln. It was a baseball tragedy from a New York point of view. The Cubs won by the score of 4 to 2.

Behind this game is some "inside" history that has never been written. Few persons, outside of the members of the New York club, know that it was only after a great deal of consultation the game was finally played, only after the urging of John T. Brush, the president of the club. The Giants were risking, in one afternoon, their chances of winning the pennant and the world's series—the concentration of their hopes of a season—because the Cubs claimed the right on a technicality to play this one game for the championship. Many members of the New York club felt that it would be fighting for what they had already won, as did their supporters. This made bad feeling between the teams and between the spectators, until the whole dramatic situation leading up to the famous game culminated in the climax of that afternoon. The nerves of the players were rasped raw with the strain, and the town wore a fringe of nervous prostration. It all burst forth in the game.

Among other things, Frank Chance, the manager of the Cubs, had a cartilage in his neck broken when some rooter hit him with a handy pop bottle, several spectators hurt one another when they switched from conversational to fistic arguments, large portions of the fence at the Polo Grounds were broken down by patrons who insisted on gaining entrance, and most of the police of New York were present to keep order. They had their clubs unlimbered, too, acting more as if on strike duty than restraining the spectators at a pleasure park. Last of all, that night, after we had lost the game, the report filtered through New York that Fred Merkle, then a youngster and around whom the whole situation revolved, had committed suicide. Of course it was not true, for Merkle is one of the gamest ball-players that ever lived.

Christy Mathewson won 373 games, the third-highest total in major league history, but suffered the loss in a one-game playoff against the Chicago Cubs to decide the 1908 National League pennant. *By Charles M. Conlon via Wikimedia Commons.*

My part in the game was small. I started to pitch and I didn't finish. The Cubs beat me because I never had less on the ball in my life. What I can't understand to this day is why it took them so long to hit me. Frequently it has been said that "Cy" Seymour started the Cubs on their victorious way and lost the game, because he misjudged a long hit jostled to centre field by "Joe" Tinker at the beginning of the third inning, in which chapter they made four runs. The hit went for three bases.

Seymour, playing centre field, had a bad background against which to judge fly balls that afternoon, facing the shadows of the towering stand, with the uncertain horizon formed by persons perched on the roof. A baseball writer has said that, when Tinker came to the bat in that fatal inning, I turned in the box and motioned Seymour back, and instead of obeying instructions he crept a few steps closer to the infield. I don't recall giving any advice to "Cy," as he knew the Chicago batters as well as I did and how to play for them.

Tinker, with his long bat, swung on a ball intended to be a low curve over the outside corner of the plate, but it failed to break well. He pushed out a high fly to centre field, and I turned with the ball to see Seymour take a couple of steps toward the diamond, evidently thinking it would drop somewhere behind second base. He appeared to be uncertain in his judgment of the hit until he suddenly turned and started to run back. That must have been when the ball cleared the roof of the stand and was visible above the sky line. He ran wildly. Once he turned, and then ran on again, at last sticking up his hands and having the ball fall just beyond them. He chased it and picked it up, but Tinker had reached third base by that time. If he had let the ball roll into the crowd in centre field, the Cub could have made only two bases on the hit, according to the ground rules. That was a mistake, but it made little difference in the end.

All the players, both the Cubs and the Giants, were under a terrific strain that day, and Seymour, in his anxiety to be sure to catch the ball, misjudged it. Did you ever stand out in the field at a ball park with thirty thousand crazy, shouting fans looking at you and watch a ball climb and climb into the air and have to make up your mind exactly where it is going to land and then have to be there, when it arrived, to greet it, realizing all the time that if you are not there you are going to be everlastingly roasted? It is no cure for nervous diseases, that situation. Probably forty-nine times out of fifty Seymour would have caught the fly.

"I misjudged that ball," said "Cy" to me in the clubhouse after the game. "I'll take the blame for it."

He accepted all the abuse the newspapers handed him without a murmur and I don't think myself that it was more than an incident in the game. I'll try to show later in this story where the real "break" came.

Just one mistake, made by "Fred" Merkle, resulted in this play-off game. Several newspaper men have called September 23, 1908, "Merkle Day," because it was on that day he ran to the clubhouse from first base instead of by way of second, when "Al" Bridwell whacked out the hit that apparently won the game from the Cubs. Any other player on the team would have undoubtedly done the same thing under the circumstances, as the custom had been in vogue all around the circuit during the season. It was simply Fred Merkle's misfortune to have been on first base at the critical moment. The situation which gave rise to the incident is well known to every follower of baseball. Merkle, as a pinch hitter, had singled with two out in the ninth inning and the score tied, sending McCormick from first base to third. "Al" Bridwell came up to the bat and smashed a single to centre field. McCormick crossed the plate, and that, according to the customs of the League, ended the game, so Merkle dug for the clubhouse. Evers and Tinker ran through the crowd which had flocked on the field and got the ball, touching second and claiming that Merkle had been forced out there.

Most of the spectators did not understand the play, as Merkle was under the shower bath when the alleged put-out was made, but they started after "Hank" O'Day, the umpire, to be on the safe side. He made a speedy departure under the grand-stand and the crowd got the put-out unassisted. Finally, while somewhere near Coogan's Bluff, he called Merkle out and the score a tie. When the boys heard this in the clubhouse, they laughed, for it didn't seem like a situation to be taken seriously. But it turned out to be one of those things that the farther it goes the more serious it becomes.

"Connie" Mack, the manager of the Athletics, says:

"There is no luck in Big League baseball In a schedule of one hundred and fifty-four games, the lucky and unlucky plays break about even, except in the matter of injuries."

But Mack's theory does not include a schedule of one hundred and fifty-five games, with the result depending on the one hundred and fifty-fifth. Chicago had a lot of injured athletes early in the season of 1908, and the Giants had shot out ahead in the race in grand style. In the meantime the Cubs' cripples began to recuperate, and that lamentable event on September 23 seemed to be the turning-point in the Giants' fortunes.

Almost within a week afterwards, Bresnahan had an attack of sciatic rheumatism and "Mike" Donlin was limping about the outfield, leading a great case of "Charley horse." Tenney was bandaged from his waist down and should have been wearing crutches instead of playing first base on a Big League club. Doyle was badly spiked and in the hospital. McGraw's daily greeting to his athletes when he came to the park was:

"How are the cripples? Any more to add to the list of identified dead to-day?"

Merkle moped. He lost flesh, and time after time begged McGraw to send him to a minor league or to turn him loose altogether,

"It wasn't your fault," was the regular response of the manager who makes it a habit to stand by his men.

We played on with the cripples, many double-headers costing the pitchers extra effort, and McGraw not daring to take a chance on losing a game if there were any opportunity to win it. He could not rest any of his men. Merkle lost weight and seldom spoke to the other players as the Cubs crept up on us day after day and more men were hurt. He felt that he was responsible for this change in the luck of the club. None of the players felt this way toward him, and many tried to cheer him up, but he was inconsolable. The team went over to Philadelphia, and Coveleski, the pitcher we later drove out of the League, beat us three times, winning the last game by the scantiest of margins. The result of that series left us three to play with Boston to tie the Cubs if they won from Pittsburg the next day, Sunday. If the Pirates had taken that Sunday game, it would have given them the pennant. We returned to New York on Saturday night very much downhearted.

"Lose me. I'm the jinx," Merkle begged McGraw that night.

"You stick," replied the manager.

While we had been losing, the Cubs had been coming fast. It seemed as if they could not drop a game. At last Cincinnati beat them one, which was the only thing that made the famous season tie possible. There is an interesting anecdote connected with that Cincinnati contest which goes to prove the honesty of baseball. Two of the closest friends in the game are "Hans" Lobert, then with the Reds, and Overall, the former Chicago pitcher. It looked as if Chicago had the important game won up to the ninth inning when Lobert came to the bat with two men out and two on the bases. Here he had a chance to overcome the lead of one run which the Cubs had gained, and win the contest for the home club, but he would beat his best friend and maybe put the Cubs out of the running for the pennant.

Lobert had two balls and two strikes when he smashed the next pitch to center field, scoring both the base runners. The hit came near beating the Cubs out of the championship. It would have if we had taken one of those close games against Philadelphia. Lobert was brokenhearted over his hit, for he wanted the Cubs to win. On his way to the clubhouse, he walked with Overall, the two striding side by side like a couple of mourners.

"I'm sorry, 'Orvie,'" said Lobert. "I would not have made that hit for my year's salary if I could have helped it."

"That's all right, 'Hans,'" returned Overall. "It's all part of the game."

Next came the famous game in Chicago on Sunday between the Cubs and the Pittsburg Pirates, when a victory for the latter club would have meant the pennant and the big game would never have been played. Ten thousand persons crowded into the Polo Grounds that Sunday afternoon and watched a little electric score board which showed the plays as made in Chicago. For the first time in my life I heard a New York crowd cheering the Cubs with great fervor, for on their victory hung our only chances of ultimate success. The same man who was shouting himself hoarse for the Cubs that afternoon was for taking a vote on the desirability of poisoning the whole Chicago team on the following Thursday. Even the New York players were rooting for the Cubs.

The Chicago team at last won the game when Clarke was called out at third base on a close play, late in the contest. With the decision, the Pirates' last chance went glimmering. The Giants now had three games to win from Boston on Monday, Tuesday and Wednesday, to make the deciding game on Thursday necessary. We won those, and the stage was cleared for the big number.

The National Commission gave the New York club the option of playing three games out of five for the championship or risking it all on one contest. As more than half of the club was tottering on the brink of the hospital, it was decided that all hope should be hung on one game. By this time, Merkle had lost twenty pounds, and his eyes were hollow and his cheeks sunken. The newspapers showed him no mercy, and the fans never failed to criticise and hiss him when he appeared on the field. He stuck to it and showed up in the ball park every day, putting on his uniform and practising. It was a game thing to do. A lot of men, under the same fire, would have quit cold. McGraw was with him all the way.

But it was not until after considerable discussion that it was decided to play that game. All the men felt disgruntled because they believed they would be playing for something they had already won. Even McGraw was so wrought up, he said in the clubhouse the night before the game:

"I don't care whether you fellows play this game or not. You can take a vote."

A vote was taken, and the players were not unanimous, some protesting it ought to be put up to the League directors so that, if they wanted to rob the team of a pennant, they would have to take the blame. Others insisted it would look like quitting, and it was finally decided to appoint a committee to call upon Mr. Brush, the president of the club, who was ill in bed in the Lambs club at the time. Devlin, Bresnahan, Donlin, Tenney, and I were on that committee.

"Mr. Brush," I said to my employer, having been appointed the spokesman, "McGraw has left it up to us to decide whether we shall meet the Chicago team for the championship of the National League to-morrow. A lot of the boys do not believe we ought to be forced to play over again for something we have already won, so the players have appointed this committee of five to consult with you and get your opinion on the subject. What we decide goes with them."

Mr. Brush looked surprised. I was nervous, more so than when I am in the box with three on the bases and "Joe" Tinker at the bat. Bresnahan fumbled with his hat, and Devlin coughed. Tenney leaned more heavily on his cane, and Donlin blew his nose. We five big athletes were embarrassed in the presence of this sick man. Suddenly it struck us all at the same time that the game would have to be played to keep ourselves square with our own ideas of courage. Even if the Cubs had claimed it on a technicality, even if we had really won the pennant once, that game had to be played now. We all saw that, and it was this thin, ill man in bed who made us see it even before he had said a word. It was the expression on his face. It seemed to say, "And I had confidence in you, boys, to do the right thing."

"I'm going to leave it to you," he answered. "You boys can play the game or put it up to the directors of the League to decide as you want. But I shouldn't think you would stop now after making all this fight."

The committee called an executive session, and we all thought of the crowd of fans looking forward to the game and of what the newspapers would say if we refused to play it and of Mr. Brush lying there, the man who wanted us to play, and it was rapidly and unanimously decided to imitate "Steve" Brodie and take a chance.

"We'll play," I said to Mr. Brush.

"I'm glad," he answered. "And, say, boys," he added, as we started to file out, "I want to tell you something. Win or lose, I'm going to give the players a bonus of $10,000."

That night was a wild one in New York. The air crackled with excitement and baseball. I went home, but couldn't sleep for I live near the Polo Grounds, and the crowd began to gather there early in the evening of the day before the game to be ready for the opening of the gates the next morning. They tooted horns all night, and were never still. When I reported at the ball park, the gates had been closed by order of the National Commission, but the streets for blocks around the Polo Grounds were jammed with persons fighting to get to the entrances.

The players in the clubhouse had little to say to one another, but, after the bandages were adjusted, McGraw called his men around him and said:

"Chance will probably pitch Pfiester or Brown. If Pfiester works there is no use trying to steal. He won't give you any lead. The right-handed batters ought to wait him out and the left-handers hit him when he gets in a hole. Matty is going to pitch for us."

Pfiester is a left-hand pitcher who watches the bases closely.

Merkle had reported at the clubhouse as usual and had put on his uniform. He hung on the edge of the group as McGraw spoke, and then we all went to the field. It was hard for us to play that game with the crowd which was there, but harder for the Cubs. In one place, the fence was broken down, and some employees were playing a stream of water from a fire hose on the cavity to keep the crowd back. Many preferred a ducking to missing the game and ran through the stream to the lines around the field. A string of fans recklessly straddled the roof of the old grand-stand.

Every once in a while some group would break through the restraining ropes and scurry across the diamond to what appeared to be a better point of vantage. This would let a throng loose which hurried one way and another and mixed in with the players. More police had to be summoned. As I watched that half-wild multitude before the contest, I could think of three or four things I would rather do than umpire the game.

I had rested my arm four days, not having pitched in the Boston series, and I felt that it should be in pretty good condition. Before that respite, I had been in nine out of fifteen games. But as I started to warm up, the ball refused to break. I couldn't get anything on it.

"What's the matter, Rog?" I asked Bresnahan. "They won't break for me."

"It'll come as you start to work," he replied, although I could see that he, too, was worried.

John M. Ward, the old ball-player and now one of the owners of the Boston National League club, has told me since that, after working almost every day as I had been doing, it does a pitcher's arm no good to lay off for three or four days. Only a week or ten days will accomplish any results. It would have been better for me to continue to work as often as I had been doing, for the short rest only seemed to deaden my arm.

The crowd that day was inflammable. The players caught this incendiary spirit. McGinnity, batting out to our infield in practice, insisted on driving Chance away from the plate before the Cubs' leader thought his team had had its full share of the batting rehearsal. "Joe" shoved him a little, and in a minute fists were flying, although Chance and McGinnity are very good friends off the field.

Fights immediately started all around in the stands. I remember seeing two men roll from the top to the bottom of the right-field bleachers, over the heads of the rest of the spectators. And they were yanked to their feet and run out of the park by the police.

"Too bad," I said to Bresnahan, nodding my head toward the departing belligerents, "they couldn't have waited until they saw the game, anyway. I'll bet they stood outside the park all night to get in, only to be run out before it started."

I forgot the crowd, forgot the fights, and didn't hear the howling after the game started. I knew only one thing, and that was my curved ball wouldn't break for me. It surprised me that the Cubs didn't hit it far, right away, but two of them fanned in the first inning and Herzog threw out Evers. Then came our first time at bat. Pfiester was plainly nervous and hit Tenney. Herzog walked and Bresnahan fanned out, Herzog being doubled up at second because he tried to advance on a short passed ball. "Mike" Donlin whisked a double to right field and Tenney counted.

For the first time in almost a month, Merkle smiled. He was drawn up in the corner of the bench, pulling away from the rest of us as if he had some contagious disease and was quarantined. For a minute it looked as if we had them going. Chance yanked Pfiester out of the box with him protesting that he had been robbed on the decisions on balls and strikes. Brown was brought into the game and fanned Devlin. That ended the inning.

We never had a chance against Brown. His curve was breaking sharply, and his control was microscopic. We went back to the field in the second with that one run lead. Chance made the first hit of the game off me in the second, but I caught him sleeping at first base, according to Klem's decision. There was a kick, and Hofman, joining in the chorus of protests, was sent to the clubhouse.

Tinker started the third with that memorable triple which gave the Cubs their chance. I couldn't make my curve break. I didn't have anything on the ball.

"Rog," I said to Bresnahan, "I haven't got anything to-day."

"Keep at it, Matty," he replied. "We'll get them all right."

I looked in at the bench, and McGraw signalled me to go on pitching. Kling singled and scored Tinker. Brown sacrificed, sending Kling to second, and Sheckard flied out to Seymour, Kling being held on second base. I lost Evers, because I was afraid to put the ball over the plate for him, and he walked. Two were out now, and we had yet a chance to win the game as the score was only tied. But Schulte doubled, and Kling scored, leaving men on second and third bases. Still we had a Mongolian's chance with them only one run ahead of us. Frank Chance, with his under jaw set like the fender on a trolley car, caught a curved ball over the inside corner of the plate and pushed it to right field for two bases. That was the most remarkable batting performance I have ever witnessed since I have been in the Big Leagues. A right-handed hitter naturally slaps a ball over the outside edge of the plate to right field, but Chance pushed this one, on the inside, with the handle of his bat, just over Tenney's hands and on into the crowd. The hit scored Evers and Schulte and dissolved the game right there. It was the "break." Steinfeldt fanned.

None of the players spoke to one another as they went to the bench. Even McGraw was silent. We knew it was gone. Merkle was drawn up behind the water cooler. Once he said:

"It was my fault, boys."

No one answered him. Inning after inning, our batters were mowed down by the great pitching of Brown, who was never better. His control of his curved ball was marvellous, and he had all his speed. As the innings dragged by, the spectators lost heart, and the cowbells ceased to jingle, and the cheering lost its resonant ring. It was now a surly growl.

Then the seventh! We had our one glimmer of sunshine. Devlin started with a single to centre, and McCormick shoved a drive to right field. Recalling that Bridwell was more or less of a pinch hitter, Brown passed him purposely and Doyle was sent to the bat in my place. As he hobbled to the plate on his weak foot, said McGraw:

"Hit one, Larry."

The crowd broke into cheers again and was stamping its feet. The bases were full, and no one was out. Then Doyle popped up a weak foul behind the catcher. His batting eye was dim and rusty through long disuse. Kling went back for it, and some one threw a pop bottle which narrowly missed him, and another scaled a cushion. But Kling kept on and got what he went after, which was the ball. He has a habit of doing that. Tenney flied to Schulte, counting Devlin on the catch, and Tinker threw out Herzog. The game was gone. Never again did we have a chance.

It was a glum lot of players in the clubhouse. Merkle came up to McGraw and said:

"Mac, I've lost you one pennant. Fire me before I can do any more harm."

"Fire you?" replied McGraw. "We ran the wrong way of the track to-day. That's all. Next year is another season, and do you think I'm going to let you go after the gameness you've shown through all this abuse? Why you're the kind of a guy I've been lookin' for many years. I could use a carload like you. Forget this season and come around next spring.. The newspapers will have forgotten it all then. Good-by, boys." And he slipped out of the clubhouse.

"He's a regular guy," said Merkle.

Merkle has lived down that failure to touch second and proved himself to be one of the gamest players that ever stood in a diamond.

Fred Merkle's baseball card from the famous T206 White Borders set (1909–11). *By American Tobacco Company via Wikimedia Commons.*

Many times since has he vindicated himself. He is a great first baseman now, and McGraw and he are close friends. That is the "inside" story of the most important game ever played in baseball and Merkle's connection with it.

CHAPTER 13

FIVE UNFORGETTABLE DINGERS

JOSHUA SHIFRIN AND TOMMY SHEA

THE BAMBINO BREAKS HIS OWN RECORD

All summer they went back and forth. Back and forth.

If one hit a home run on Saturday, the other would slam one on Sunday. Seven times in the course of the 1927 season they hit homers in the same game.

Newspapers called it "The Great American Home Run Derby," and it starred Babe Ruth and Lou Gehrig.

Only two homers would separate them from April into September. Ruth batted third in the New York Yankees lineup, Gehrig fourth. They got used to shaking each other's hands at home plate.

The 1927 New York Yankees were arguably the best team in baseball history. Six players—Ruth, Gehrig, second baseman Tony Lazzeri, center fielder Earle Combs, and pitchers Waite Hoyt and Herb Pennock—were elected into the Hall of Fame. Their manager, Miller Huggins, became a Hall of Famer, too.

They won the American League pennant by Labor Day and would finish with 110 wins and 44 losses.

Combs, the leadoff hitter, owned a .356 average. Lazzeri and left fielder Bob Meusel knocked in more than 100 runs each. Hoyt won 22 games, Pennock earned the W in 19.

A decade earlier, the top home run hitters were Dave Robertson of the New York Giants and Gavvy Cravath of the Philadelphia Phillies. They had 12 each. (Lazzeri had 18 in 1927, third in the league and third on the Yankees.) Wally Pipp, who famously would lose his first-base job to Gehrig in 1925 after being hit by a pitch and then complaining of a headache, was third in all of baseball in 1917, with nine homers.

On August 9, Gehrig actually nudged past Ruth, 38 homers to 35.

"It was the first time anyone had directly challenged Ruth's pre-eminence," Robert Creamer wrote in his 1974 book *Babe: The Legend Comes to Life.*

Ruth, of course, was no surprise.

In 1920, his first year as a Yankee, he launched 54 bombs and changed baseball forever. The following year he slammed 59. In 1926, he rounded the bases 47 times. He failed to win the home run crown in 1922 and 1925 because he missed six and seven weeks of those respective seasons.

Gehrig was a different story.

In 1927 he was only twenty-four, eight years Ruth's junior, in the midst of his third full season in the big leagues. He was as quiet as Ruth was loud. Coming out of Columbia University, he had pounded 20 homers in 1925 and followed up with 16 in 1926, using his gap power to also leg out 20 triples.

In his 2005 book *Luckiest Man: The Life and Death of Lou Gehrig,* Jonathan Eig described Gehrig's approach at the plate: "He lowered

Babe Ruth in 1920, his first year as a New York Yankee, when he hit 54 home runs. *By Paul Thompson via Wikimedia Commons.*

his center of gravity when he swung so that his left knee almost scraped the ground. He didn't need to flail. Ruth, with his wild, up-from-the-heels swing, hit soaring rockets that disappeared high in the air and fell to earth often in bleachers. Gehrig swung from the shoulder, as if wielding an ax. His home runs seemed to zip just over the second baseman's head and continue rising until they banged off a seat in the right field bleachers. His shots almost seemed to whistle."

Gehrig told *Baseball Magazine* in 1927 he didn't consider himself a home run hitter.

"I have as much respect for a home run as anybody, but I like straightaway hitting. I believe it's the proper way to hit. If a fellow has met the ball just right on the nose, he's done what he set out to do."

In 1927, while competing against his hero and friend Ruth for the home run championship, and maybe even a new home run record, Gehrig also delivered 52 doubles, piled up 173 RBIs, and put up a .373 average.

Ruth and Gehrig were tied in homers on September 6 when the Yankees played the lousy Boston Red Sox (they'd lose 103 games, the third straight season of 100 or more losses) in a doubleheader at Fenway Park.

Leigh Montville, in his 2006 bestseller *The Big Bam: The Life and Times of Babe Ruth,* set the scene: "In the fifth inning of the first game, Tony Welzer on the mound for the Sox, Gehrig unloaded a shot into the right field bleachers to take the lead at 45. . . .

"In the sixth, Ruth came back at him. With two men on base, Welzer tried a change of pace on the Bam. The Bam was waiting for it. He ran up on the ball and, according to the *New York Times,* 'dealt the sphere a fearful blow,' a shot instantly considered the longest homer in Fenway history. . . .

"In the next inning, poor Welzer still on the mound, Ruth connected again. This was a tall fly ball that sneaked into the stands close to the right field pole. Ruth 46, Gehrig 45. Finally, in the seventh inning of the nightcap, Ruth broke up Charlie Russell's shutout with another fly ball down the right field line that snuck into the stands. Gehrig, the next batter, followed with a shot to left center, longer and harder hit than Ruth's homer that stayed in the park for a triple.

"And, yet somehow just like that the chase was done."

There were 22 games left in the season. Ruth needed 13 home runs to break his record. When he hit his 50th on September 11, he said he thought he could break his old record of 59.

It was good copy, but no one quite believed Ruth.

But he launched a grand slam off Philadelphia A's future Hall of Famer Lefty Grove on September 27. It was number 57, with four games to play.

Number 58 was off Washington's Hod Lisenbee, a skinny rookie right-hander with a funky delivery. He'd once struck out Ruth three times in a single game. In 1927, he led the American League with four shutouts and was 18–9.

None of that mattered to Ruth. In the first inning of the 152nd game of the season, Ruth, with two strikes, whacked a Lisenbee pitch into the right- field bleachers.

In the fifth, with the bases loaded, Washington manager Bucky Harris called upon twenty-five-year-old Paul Hopkins to make his major-league debut against Babe Ruth.

Ruth hit two long foul balls. The count was 3 and 2. Hopkins's next thought was that he'd snap off a deceptive curveball.

"Real slow and over the outside of the plate," Hopkins said almost seventy years later to a *Sports Illustrated* reporter. "It was so slow that Ruth started to swing and then hesitated. He hitched on it and brought the bat back. And then he swung, breaking his wrists as he came through. What a great eye he had! He hit it at the right second. Put everything behind it. I can still hear the crack of the bat. I can still see the swing."

Ruth had tied his record of 59 home runs.

The following day, September 30, a Friday at Yankee Stadium, Ruth knocked in both Yankee runs on singles. The game was tied 2–2 in the eighth.

Tom Zachary was pitching for the Senators. He was left-handed and he threw hard. He would win 186 games in his 19-year big-league career. And he would give up nine career homers to Ruth.

Mark Koenig, a terrific Yankee shortstop, was on third. Zachary's first pitch to Ruth was a strike. The second pitch was high. The third was stroked high and deep to right.

Zachary threw his glove to the ground and barked at the umpires that the ball was foul.

Ruth had bopped his 17th homer of the month and 60th of the season. He delighted in making his way around the bases, waving his cap to the 8,000 or so in attendance.

At home plate, Gehrig was there to congratulate Ruth with a hearty handshake and a pat on the back.

The next day, October 1, the last game of the regular season, Ruth went homerless.

Gehrig hit his 47th. No one made a big deal of it.

Gehrig was named the American League Most Valuable Player.

But Ruth had become only more legendary.

WILLIE MAYS'S CLASSIC CLOUT OFF OF SPAHN

In 22 seasons, Willie Mays played in 24 All-Star Games, hit 660 home runs, and collected a total of 3,283 hits. For eight consecutive seasons, from 1959 to 1966, he knocked in 100 runs. In 1954 and 1965 he was named the National League Most Valuable Player. He made a catch in the 1954 World Series that will be remembered as long as there is baseball. He also won 12 Gold Gloves—and the award didn't exist until his sixth season, 1957—in the big leagues for his fielding prowess. He should have been unanimously elected to the Hall of Fame. (He wasn't, securing 409 votes out of the potential 432 baseball writer ballots.) He was the 10th black player to make the big leagues.

When he was brought to the New York Giants in 1951, Mays was hitting .477 for Minneapolis in Triple A.

He struck out in his first at-bat and went 0-for-his-first-12 against the Philadelphia Phillies at Shibe Park in the City of Brotherly Love, but the Giants—17–19 when he was called to the majors—won three in a row with him in the lineup.

The next day, May 28, in New York, at the Polo Grounds, before 23,101 fans, Mays batted third.

In the first inning, Eddie Stanky walked before Whitey Lockman hit into a double play against future Hall of Famer Warren Spahn, pitching for the Boston Braves. Up came Mays. He was twenty.

Giants scout Montague told Tim Cohane, the sports editor of *Look* magazine, that he been scouting Alonzo Perry, a teammate of Mays with the Negro League's Birmingham Black Barons in 1948, but he couldn't take his eyes off the center fielder, Mays.

"This was the greatest young player I had ever seen in my life or my scouting career," he wrote, upon seeing Mays.

Durocher, in his book *Nice Guys Finish Last*, described Mays this way: "If somebody came up and hit .450, stole 100 bases, and performed a miracle in the field every day, I'd still look you right in the eye and tell you that Willie was better. He could do the five things you have to do to be a superstar: hit, hit with power, run, throw, and field. And he had the other magic ingredient that turns a superstar into a super Superstar. Charisma. He lit up a room when he came in. He was a joy to be around."

But on May 28, 1951, Mays was still a prospect, all promise.

Spahn, who won 363 games, more than any left-handed pitcher in the history of baseball, remembers facing Mays for the first time.

"I'll never forgive myself. We might have gotten rid of Willie forever if I'd only struck him out," he told a reporter in jest. He noted that the pitcher's mound is 60 feet, 6 inches from home plate, and his pitch to the rookie looked like "a helluva pitch" for 60 feet.

Mays launched the ball over the roof in left.

He then went hitless in his next 13 at-bats, making Mays 1-for-26. According to legend, after the game he was caught crying in front of his locker, telling Durocher he couldn't hit major-league pitching.

Durocher said, "As long as I'm the manager of the Giants you are my center fielder. . . . You are the best center fielder I've ever looked at."

Mays went 14 for his next 33. He slugged 20 homers as a rookie in 1951, the year the Giants made their remarkable comeback to win the National League pennant on Bobby Thomson's home run. Mays was on deck when that ball soared into history.

Mays missed the next year and a half because of military obligations but returned in 1954 to hit .345 with 41 home runs, leading the Giants to the world championship.

Mays would hit 18 career homers off Spahn, the most he would hit off any pitcher. (He also slugged 13 off another Hall of Fame pitcher, the Dodgers' Don Drysdale.)

His most famous home run off Spahn came in 1963. The Giants were based in San Francisco, at homer-unfriendly Candlestick Park, where the damp wind tended to blow in.

On July 2, a Tuesday night, Spahn, forty-two, took the hill for the Milwaukee Braves. He had spun a three-hit shutout four days earlier against the Dodgers. Two years before that, in 1961, he had no-hit the Giants, his second career no-no.

Juan Marichal, twenty-five, was pitching for the Giants. Seventeen days earlier, Marichal had thrown a no-hitter against Houston.

Spahn, who had won his 300th game in 1961, was on his way to a 23–7 record with 22 complete games, his last great season.

Bud Selig, the future commissioner of baseball, making his first trip to San Francisco, was in attendance, rooting for his hometown Braves. He couldn't believe how cold San Francisco could be in July.

On that chilly evening, Marichal and Spahn both threw zeroes, inning after inning after inning after inning, in one of the greatest pitching duels in baseball history.

Mays threw a runner out at the plate in the fourth. The Giants' Willie McCovey nearly hit a home run in the ninth, but the ball went foul.

Both pitchers worked out of mild jams.

Giants manager Alvin Dark wanted to take Marichal out in the 9th, 12th, and 15th innings, but the young pitcher—in the midst of his breakout season—kept talking him out of it.

Spahn kept grabbing a bat when it was his turn to hit. His manager, Bobby Bragan, decided it was Spahn's game to win or lose.

After 16 innings, Marichal had allowed eight hits and four walks. He struck out 10. He allowed no runs. The only extra-base hit was a double by Spahn in the seventh. Along with being a great pitcher,

Spahn was also a good hitter. He would hit 35 career home runs and once hit .333 in a season.

Entering the bottom of the 16th, Spahn's pitching line was eight hits allowed and one walk.

The game featured McCovey and Milwaukee's Hank Aaron, twenty-nine, who would lead the National League in home runs with 44 each; the Giants' Harvey Kuenn, a former American League batting champion; and future Hall of Famers Eddie Mathews of the Braves and Orlando Cepeda of the Giants.

And, of course, Willie Mays, who had gone 0-for-5 with a walk when he stepped to the plate with one out in the bottom of the 16th.

Mays had this habit of always stepping on first base at home after an inning. He followed his usual script on July 2 after the top of the 16th. Marichal was waiting for him.

"When he got there, I put my arm on his shoulder and I told him, 'Alvin Dark is mad at me. He's not going to let me pitch any longer,'" Marichal recounted to the *San Jose Mercury News* on the 50th anniversary of the game.

"So [Mays] touched my back and said, 'Don't worry. I'm going to win this game for you.'"

And he did. A long drive that cleared the fence in left. The Giants won, 1–0.

Marichal fired an incredible 227 pitches, mostly fastballs, in the game. Spahn mixed it up but threw 201 pitches.

The next day, the *San Francisco Chronicle* quoted Spahn as saying he threw Mays a screwball that "didn't break worth a damn."

In his next start, Spahn tossed a shutout to beat Houston.

Marichal would finish the season with 25 wins. He threw 321 1/3 innings that year, a massive total.

Winning pitcher Juan Marichal congratulates Willie Mays (right) on his game-win-ning home run in the 16th inning to beat Warren Spahn and the Milwaukee Braves, 1-0, on July 2, 1963. *AP Photo.*

Mays added 38 homers to his lifetime totals.

In 1968, he would hit a 15th-inning home run off Cincinnati's Ted Abernathy, which set another baseball record: most innings in which a player hit a home run. Mays, who retired in 1973 at forty-two, still holds the mark: 16.

THE MICK'S FAVORITE BLAST

Mickey Mantle was a lot of things, but there was one thing he wasn't: a braggart.

Standing in the on-deck circle with Elston Howard, watching right-handed knuckleball specialist Barney Schultz finish his warmup pitches on October 10, 1964 (a Saturday afternoon World Series game at Yankee Stadium), Mantle turned to his teammate and said, "You can go back to the clubhouse, Elston. This game is over."

In the dugout, getting a drink of water after pitching nine terrific innings, Yankee starter Jim Bouton saw Mantle holding his bat.

"He was standing there with his bat on his shoulder, watching Barney Schultz. His warm-up pitches were coming in about thigh high and breaking down to the shin, to the ankles—two or three in a row. Mickey said, 'I'm gonna hit one outta here.' It wasn't a big announcement. He wasn't like that. He wasn't a grandstander. He might have been saying it to himself. He understood that Barney Schultz was the wrong guy for them to bring in."

The New York Yankees and St. Louis Cardinals had split the first two games of the World Series and were tied, 1–1, in the bottom of the ninth of Game Three. A Mantle error in right field led to the only Cardinal run. It really bothered him.

"By that time I couldn't run too much anymore," he told author Jane Leavy, biographer of Sandy Koufax and Mantle, in 1983. "They put me in right field and [Roger] Maris in center. Somebody hit me a groundball. I nonchalanted it. It went through my legs, and the guy scored."

St. Louis hurler Curt Simmons matched Bouton pitch for pitch.

In his eight innings, Simmons, a crafty veteran left-hander who had missed pitching in the World Series for the 1950 Philadelphia Phillies "Whiz Kids" because of military obligations, had the Yankees hitting the ball into the ground, forcing 17 ground-ball outs. Bouton, a fireballing right-hander who would became more famous six years later for writing the candid book *Ball Four*, stranded the go-ahead runner four times. He held the top five hitters (Curt Flood, Lou Brock, Bill White, Ken Boyer, and Dick Groat) in the Cardinals lineup to two hits.

Barney Schultz was a big reason why the Cardinals won the National League pennant. The thirty-eight-year-old journeyman saved 14 games down the stretch, pitching in 30 of the final 60 regular-season games, helping the Cardinals overtake the collapsing Philadelphia Phillies, who let a 6 1/2-game lead with 12 to play wither away.

Schultz, who owned a 1.64 ERA, had given up one homer all season. He was pitching in his first World Series. He earned the save in Game One.

The Yankees had been in third place in the American League on August 22—and looking old.

Rookie pitcher Mel Stottlemyre, who won nine games in only 12 starts that season, was a huge help. So was the September 5 acquisition from Cleveland of reliever Pedro Ramos, who saved eight games down the stretch.

Catcher Elston Howard hit nearly .400 in the final weeks of the season. Maris was a key late-stage force at the plate and in the field. Twenty-three-year-old first baseman Joe Pepitone came alive offensively, hitting 12 homers and knocking in 30 runs in the heat of a pennant race.

Mantle slugged seven homers in September, as the Yankees won 27 of their final 35 games, capturing the American League title by one game, their 14th pennant in 16 years.

Mantle, about to turn thirty-three, had his last great season in 1964: 33 homers, 111 RBIs, .303 batting average, and an OPS of 1.015.

In the ninth inning of Game Three of the World Series, the score tied 1–1, the game's greatest switch-hitter stepped into the left-handed batter's box, number 7 on his back. The crowd of 67,000 at Yankee Stadium stood with expectation.

While Mantle had hit .300 in '64 for the 10th time and had homered more than 30 times for the ninth season of a career that began in 1951, his batting average from the left side was only .241 that season. The Cardinals knew this.

Tim McCarver, the Cardinals' twenty-two-year-old catcher, later told author Jane Leavy that he also knew Mantle, with knee and shoulder woes, was struggling, "a shell of the player that he once was. I could even hear him groaning on some swings. A swing and a miss were real bad."

The first pitch from Schultz, McCarver said, was a knuckler that "dangled like bait to a big fish. Plus it lingered in that area that was down, and Mickey was a lethal low-ball hitter left-handed. The pitch was so slow that it allowed him to turn on it and pull it."

Mantle hit it so high and so far that Bouton thought it was going to be the first home run slugged out of Yankee Stadium.

It wasn't, although it landed deep in the third deck.

With his 16th World Series home run, Mantle surpassed Babe Ruth as the all-time leader.

At the time, Mantle was only the fifth to hit a walk-off home run—the others were Tommy Henrich of the 1949 Yankees, Dusty Rhodes of the 1954 New York Giants, Eddie Mathews of the 1957 Milwaukee Braves, and Bill Mazeroski of the 1960 Pittsburgh Pirates—in World Series history.

As usual, Mantle circled the bases with his head down. After he had crossed home plate and was drenched by champagne in the

Mickey Mantle is congratulated by third-base coach Frank Crosetti on his game-winning home run against the St. Louis Cardinals in Game Three of the 1964 World Series. *AP Photo.*

clubhouse, he was asked by reporters how many other homers he had called in his career.

"I called them about 500 times," Mantle said with a laugh. "That was the only time I did it. Usually, I struck out."

His first walk-off home run came against the Red Sox in 1953. He would hit 13 in his career (12 in the regular season), his last coming off Detroit's Fred Gladding on June 24, 1967, at Yankee Stadium.

Mantle would later say the homer off Schultz was the highlight of his career, one that would include 536 home runs.

Mantle would hit his 17th homer in Game Six off Simmons, a Yankee win, and give the Yanks a chance with his 18th in Game Seven, off Bob Gibson, but the Cardinals, his favorite team as a kid growing up in Commerce, Oklahoma, won the World Series.

It was the first time the Yankees had lost back-to-back World Series since 1921–22, when they bowed to the New York Giants.

In his final World Series, Mantle hit .333. Only Yogi Berra would play in more Fall Classics.

Mantle played in 12 World Series and hit more homers and drove in more runs (40) than anyone in baseball history.

HANK AARON: 715

Henry Louis "Hank" Aaron was a Depression-era baby, born on February 5, 1934, in Mobile, Alabama. Affected by the disastrous economy of that era, his parents, Herbert and Estella, struggled to make ends meet, forcing the young Henry and his seven siblings to spend much of their youth picking cotton. But despite their financial woes, the Aaron family loved their baseball. The boys honed their batting skills by hitting bottle caps with sticks, and this unique approach apparently paid dividends as both Henry and his brother Tommie went on to play Major League Baseball. Each established solid reputations, both as players and men of character, but Hank truly left a legacy for the ages.

After a stint playing with the Indianapolis Clowns of the Negro Leagues, Aaron would make his major-league debut on April 13, 1954, with the Milwaukee Braves. In total, Hammerin' Hank played for 23 seasons. And by the time he had retired, he had compiled a staggering list of accomplishments:

Major-league record for the most career runs batted in (RBIs) with 2,297.

Major-league record of 1,477 extra-base hits.

Major-league record of 6,856 total bases.

3,771 career hits, placing him third on the all-time list.

National League's Most Valuable Player in 1957.

Three Gold Glove Awards.

The only player in the history of the game to hit 30 home runs in a season at least 15 times.

Seventeen consecutive seasons with at least 150 hits, another major-league record.

All-Star team selection every year from 1955 through 1975.

And that other thing . . . Hammerin' Hank launched a career total of 755 home runs!

But clearly, Aaron had one dinger that stands apart from the rest. As he began to draw closer to Babe Ruth's "unobtainable" mark of 714 career home runs, he tried to downplay the excitement. But as the sporting world clamored for news of every at bat, the achievement in the making took on a life of its own.

Unfortunately, there was a sinister element at play in those years. In the early 1970s, racial tension in the United States still ran high. Many fans took offense to the notion that one of the most hallowed milestones in baseball was going to be broken by a black man. To add to the strain, when Aaron ended the 1973 season, he was still sitting on 713 homers, one behind the Babe.

During the ensuing off-season, Aaron received tremendous support, but he received many death threats, as well. At one point he publicly wondered if he would survive until the following spring. But as the 1974 season began, Aaron seemed to brush off the overwhelming pressure of the moment, and he dramatically homered off of Jack Billingham in Cincinnati in his first at-bat of the season. This tied him with Babe Ruth at 714.

A few days later, Aaron and the Braves returned home. The date was April 8, 1974. A record crowd of 53,775 came to Atlanta's Fulton County Stadium.

Hank Aaron holds up the ball he hit for his 715th home run on April 8, 1974. *AP Photo.*

The long-anticipated moment occurred in the fourth inning. To the delight of the roaring crowd, Aaron smacked a pitch from Los Angeles Dodgers hurler Al Downing into the center bullpen. Broadcaster Vin Scully offered an elegant account:

"What a marvelous moment for baseball; what a marvelous moment for Atlanta and the state of Georgia; what a marvelous moment for the country and the world. A black man is getting a standing ovation in the Deep South for breaking a record of an all-time baseball idol. And it is a great moment for all of us, and particularly for Henry Aaron. . . . And for the first time in a long time, that poker face in Aaron shows the tremendous strain and relief of what it must have been like to live with for the past several months."

Aaron would end his career with 755 home runs. Although Barry Bonds has since surpassed the mark, many fans still regard Aaron as the true home run king because of the steroid cloud that hovers over Bonds.

On August 1, 1982, Aaron was enshrined into the Baseball Hall of Fame with 97.8% of the votes, second only to Ty Cobb's 98.2% at the time, and it speaks volumes about the richly deserved respect accorded to one of the classiest gentlemen to ever play the game.

KIRK GIBSON: WOUNDED WARRIOR

Kirk Harold Gibson was born in Pontiac, Michigan, on May 28, 1957, and grew up in Waterford, Michigan. As a youth, he was an outstanding all-around athlete. Gibson's baseball career was more of an afterthought than an original goal.

After attending Michigan State University and playing wide receiver for the football team, his All-American status gave him a real chance at the National Football League. At the suggestion of his football coach, Darryl Rogers, Gibson decided to play collegiate baseball, as well. And while Gibson played only one year of college baseball, he hit .390 with 16 dingers and 52 RBIs in only 48 games. Eventually, this dual threat was drafted by both the Detroit Tigers baseball team (first round), and the St. Louis Cardinals football team (seventh round). Luckily for the baseball fans of the world, Gibson chose the diamond over the gridiron. And on September 8, 1979, Kirk Gibson made his major-league debut for the Tigers.

Gibson's decision to play professional baseball turned out to be well advised. By the time he concluded his playing career, Gibson was a two-time World Series champion (1984 and 1988), the National League Most Valuable Player (1988), and the American League Championship Series Most Valuable Player (1984). But he will be remembered most for his heroics in the 1988 World Series.

As members of the Los Angeles Dodgers, Gibson and his teammates were the underdogs as they faced the powerful Oakland Athletics in the 1988 World Series. Having injured both legs during the National League Championship Series, and fighting a stomach virus to boot, Gibson was not expected to play.

In Game One, playing in front of their home crowd, the Dodgers were trailing by a run in the bottom of the ninth. Mike Davis was on first, and Los Angeles was down to its final out. It was at this point that Dodgers manager Tommy Lasorda called on the hobbled Gibson to pinch-hit against Oakland's Hall of Fame closer Dennis Eckersley.

Eck quickly got Gibson down in the count, 0–2. Gibson laid off the next two outside pitches. After Gibson fouled off a pitch, and then ran the count full, Eckersley was again ready to fire. With the crowd in frenzy, the pitch came in. With an awkward upper body swipe, Kirk

Kirk Gibson celebrates his game-winning home run against the Oakland Athletics in Game One of the 1988 World Series. *AP Photo/Rusty Kennedy.*

took the backdoor slider over the right-field fence and proceeded with a gimpy trot around the bases, pumping his fist to the jubilation of the crowd. The Dodgers would take the momentum from this 5–4 victory and run away with the title, four games to one.

After his playing career came to an end, Gibson worked as a broadcaster before returning to the dugout to manage and coach. He was named the National League Manager of the Year in 2011, with the Arizona Diamondbacks.

CHAPTER 14

GAME SIX

GREG W. PRINCE

I was sure the Mets would win Game Six of the 1986 World Series as it began on Saturday night, October 25.

I was sure of it when some dude named Michael Sergio parachuted into Shea Stadium, wielding a "Let's Go Mets" banner. He got arrested.

I was sure of it when Roger Clemens began mowing down Mets batters, not giving up a hit for four innings. When it came to generating offense, they couldn't get arrested.

I was sure of it when the Red Sox bolted to a 2–0 lead off Ojeda. Ojeda, quick deficits, and Game Sixes were already a proven combination.

I was sure of it when the Mets broke through in the fifth, beginning with a Strawberry walk and steal, followed by a Knight single to score Darryl and a Mookie single that, combined with a Dwight Evans error in right, put Ray on third.

I was sure of it when Danny Heep ground into a double play, scoring Knight to tie it at two. It wasn't the most optimal at bat, but he wasn't a dunner anymore.

I was sure of it when Knight threw a ball out of Hernandez's reach on a grounder, setting up the lead run in the seventh. These things happen.

I was sure of it when Mookie threw out Jim Rice at home from left for the third out of the seventh. Mookie wasn't a left fielder by trade. And he didn't have that great an arm.

I was sure of it when erstwhile Met Calvin Schiraldi, part of the package that brought us Ojeda, replaced Clemens. Clemens was done in more by a blister than the Mets. Schiraldi had emerged as Boston's closer late in the season. A whiny talk show caller had weeks earlier predicted the Series would end with Calvin Schiraldi striking out Gary Carter. Nonsense.

I was sure of it when erstwhile ex-Met Lee Mazzilli led off the bottom of the eighth with a pinch single. Mazz returned to Shea in August, reborn from 1979 and all those rancid, empty years, scooped up from the scrap heap after the last-place Pirates released him. George Foster, who was supposed to usher in a post-Mazzilli era of success, got on management's last nerve when he charged them with racism for sitting him down (never mind his color-blind .227 average). Mazz, like Seaver in '83, like Rusty in '81, returned to where he belonged. Mazz had better timing.

I was sure of it when the bases were loaded with one out and Gary Carter took a mighty swing against Schiraldi and it was enough to score Mazz from third on a sac fly. We were tied, 3–3.

I was sure of it when Knight and Mookie got on to start the bottom of the ninth . . . maybe less so when HoJo—whom Davey didn't order to bunt more than once—struck out and Mazz, then Dykstra each flied out. One of those fly balls would have scored Knight, theoretically, but who's to say those fly balls would have been hit had HoJo gotten a bunt down? Or that Mazzilli, still in the game in a double switch that famously annoyed Darryl because he was the one who got switched out, wouldn't have been walked to set up a double play and Lenny would have come through? On the other hand, I watched a Spring Training game that March in which HoJo laid down the most beautiful bunt I've ever seen to this day. Still, I was sure the Mets would win Game Six and stay alive to win in Game Seven even if it was going to take extra innings.

* * *

My father didn't seem to have free-floating anxieties that tended to put everybody on the edge of hysteria. His demons rarely came out to play the way my mother's did. He was the quiet one, every friend who ever came over to the house testified. He watched sports with interest and insight and enthusiasm, but except for pounding a low ceiling tile out of its socket at the Garden during a Knicks-Celtics playoff game in 1973, I'd never seen him react wildly to a game of any kind.

But I had never seen him watch the 1986 Mets on the brink of elimination before. I had never seen his superstitious side. I had never seen anybody do what he decided to for the tenth inning of Game Six. He got up from the bedroom where he was watching with my mother and went into the kitchen. He plucked a *Wall Street Journal* from his tower of unread papers and sat down at the kitchen table to leaf through it. The kitchen TV was on, but he decided that if he acted as if he didn't care what happened, nothing bad would befall the Mets.

As he pored over stock tables and I, who had been shuttling between upstairs and downstairs all night, preoccupied my antsy hands with a bowl of Grape-Nuts Flakes, Dave Henderson stepped in to lead off against Rick Aguilera, the pitcher who was part of the Mazz-Straw double switch. Aggie had pitched a scoreless ninth. He was, albeit once it barely mattered, the Mets' most effective starter for much of the regular season's second-half runaway. I was sure he'd do his part here against the Sox in the tenth, just before midnight.

Henderson homered off Aguilera.

Midnight struck. I was no longer so sure.

* * *

My father berated himself for letting the little man inside the TV know he was paying attention. My mother groaned. I discarded my Grape-Nuts Flakes and have yet to come near another bowl of the stuff since. It was bad luck. Everything was bad luck. Dave Henderson was suddenly the inverse of Steve Henderson. He had hit the most horrifying home run in the history of Shea Stadium.

All at once, 1986 was falling apart. Henderson was the big hero from the Red Sox's ALCS comeback over the Angels. Now he was doing it again. Aguilera was now the fifth starter from the first half of the season when he couldn't get the key outs. It wasn't just Henderson now. Wade Boggs came up and doubled. Marty Barrett, who'd been killing us the whole Series, singled him home. It's 5–3 instead of 4–3. It's two runs instead of one run. It's that much less surmountable now.

Bill Buckner gets hit by a pitch and goes to first. A Jim Rice flyout guarantees he's left there. But the damage is done.

* * *

Down two with three outs separating us from defeat, I decided that I needed to take in the bottom of the tenth upstairs, by myself. I headed back to my office, my sister's old bedroom. It's where I watched Ron

Swoboda double home Cleon Jones on October 16, 1969, and Swoboda score on an error thereafter and the Mets win the World Series that day. It's where a duckling was reborn a swan and where I signed on for a lifetime hitch of monitoring every Met action and reaction that followed Cleon catching that last out from Davey Johnson. It's where a little plaque that read "World Champions 1969" hung behind the TV (the Panasonic I inherited from my parents when they upgraded, the Panasonic on which I watched Steve Henderson go deep on Allen Ripley, June 14, 1980). Mark gave it to me the previous Chanukah, a consolation prize for the Mets not becoming the World Champions of 1985. Joel saw it and pronounced it sad. Not sad the Mets won in 1969. Sad the Mets hadn't won since.

I was by no means sure the Mets could come back, but I wasn't completely forlorn. We were still the '86 Mets. 108–54. Houston. Wally, Keith, and Gary due up. Who the hell was Calvin Schiraldi anyway?

* * *

I turned on the stereo in my bedroom and cranked up Bob Murphy. Back in my office down the hall, I lowered the volume on Vin Scully and Joe Garagiola. They were already spewing about how the Red Sox were on the verge of ending a sixty-eight-year drought between World Series titles and how Marty Barrett was the Miller Lite player of the game.

Shut up, Vin and Joe. If I'm going down, I'm going down with Murph.

* * *

C'mon Mets! C'mon! You've got to have two runs in you. You definitely have the right guy coming up.

Wally Backman. I love Wally Backman. There's nobody I'd rather have come up in this spot than Wally Backman. Wally Backman never lets me down. He's the most dependable guy on this team. Who got on base in Game Three against Houston to set up Dykstra? Wally, that's who. Wally is not going to allow the Mets to go down. He's going to get on. We can still do this.

WALLY! A lousy fly ball to leftfield. Jim Rice catches it. One out. Shit.

That's OK. It's just one out. We're not dead yet. Keith Hernandez is up. Keith is only the most clutch hitter in all of baseball. We've seen it all of this year and last year and the year before. Keith is the reason we're any good at all. God, I love Keith Hernandez. There is nobody I'd rather have up with everything on the line. Keith can get on. There's only one out. We can still do this.

Home run swing! Deep! But it's dying. Of course it is, it's Shea. That annoying Dave Henderson catches it in center. I hate that guy. Two out.

Shit.

*　*　*

I was sure we were doomed. I was sure the 108 wins no longer mattered. I was sure defeating Houston in Game Six was for naught. That was Game Six then. This was Game Six now. The Mets who couldn't be stopped were, in fact, one out from total stoppage. The 1986 Mets, so destined to put another plaque on the wall behind the TV, would do no more than wave a National League pennant. They did that in '73. That was fine then. You had to believe it wasn't enough now.

*　*　*

Schiraldi's unhittable. Didn't do jack for the Mets in his '84 and '85 cups of coffee, but now he's going to win the World Series for the Red Sox. Him and Dave Henderson. That fucker who called WFUV and said it would be Schiraldi on the mound to finish off Game Seven, striking out Gary Carter, he was off by one day.

The last out *is* gonna be Gary Carter.

Shit.

* * *

Fucking Carter. He's the last guy I want up there. Who made the last out last year against the Cardinals? Carter. Who hit .255 this year? Carter. Who is not going to come through in a situation like this? Carter. Can you picture him actually getting a hit here?

Carter got a hit.

Oh, why bother? Stop teasing me. I've lived through this too much as a Mets fan, all these false rallies, all this false hope in ninth innings and extra innings all my life. So Carter gets a hit. Big deal. We're still losing by two and look who's coming up.

Kevin Mitchell. Damn it, I don't want him up there.

Mitchell had a nice start this year when he made the team out of St. Petersburg and was playing all those positions, but has he done a damn thing since they went to Wrigley and he decided he was going to hit it onto Waveland Avenue every time up? I read his father was there and he wanted to impress him. Seems all he did was go into a season-long slump. Wasn't he hitting like .349 and what did he wind up at? It was .277, I think. Geez, he's a rookie who swings at everything now. This is no time for Kevin Mitchell.

Mitchell got a hit! Carter's on second!

Oh, goddamn it. Now I have to take this seriously. Why can't they just get this over with? It's as good as done anyway, probably. I hope we win, but I can't believe we will.

Look who's up. Knight.

Fantastic. Ray Knight. Perfect ending to a perfect year. Ray Knight was the *worst* player on the 1985 Mets. If he had been any good at all, or if Davey had benched him and put HoJo in like he should've, we would've beaten the fucking Cardinals last year. Instead he batted .218. I'd never booed a Met before but I couldn't help myself. Ray Knight was just so fucking awful! It was nothing personal. It was more directed at Davey for sticking with this stiff.

So this year Ray Knight makes us think everything is fine. He hits six homers in April and he hits that game-winner against the Astros on Fireworks Night and suddenly Ray Knight is a good player again. But y'know what? I don't believe it. This is all a setup. Ray Knight is going to revert to form right now. He's going to pop up or ground out or swing through one of Schiraldi's fastballs. We are so fucked and now it's worse because they're getting our fucking hopes up.

KNIGHT SINGLED! CARTER SCORED! 5–4! MITCHELL'S ON THIRD!

WE'RE ALIVE!

I can barely breathe.

* * *

It was official. 1986 no longer had to worry about being ho-hum. It took 162 regular-season games, six NLCS games, five World Series games, and nearly ten innings of this, but we were now on a par with 1985 for what we can loosely call excitement. We also reached the point where the Mets could start being the Mets for real, start being the Mets as we had always known them. It was quite gratifying to have that joyride through the National League, the mammoth lead, the whole universe anointing us favorites, and opponents seething at our greatness. But that wasn't us. Down to a final out with nobody on and reaching into the depths of our being to salvage three consecutive singles to remain extant . . . to get within one run and ninety feet of tying it and ensuring we'd continue . . . yeah, *that* was us.

I had given up. I had honestly given up. I never gave up (not counting, like, 1978) but here I had. Wally was a great chance. Keith was a great chance. They didn't happen. When they didn't, I gave up. I stopped believing.

Maybe I had to, just once, to remember what it meant to believe.

* * *

John McNamara was changing pitchers. Out went Schiraldi. In came Bob Stanley, the old Red Sox closer, the one their fans no longer liked. Kind of like us and Orosco.

Mookie Wilson's up.

Oh, this sucks.

Mookie. Of all fucking people, Mookie. Has Mookie *ever* gotten a big hit for us?

OK, I know he has. He won a game off Bruce Sutter when I was sitting in my dorm room calling Sports Phone my first semester. I thought it would propel us toward the split-season title in 1981. It didn't. And Mookie did score from second on ground balls in 1983. But Mookie *now*?

Mookie has been nothing but unfulfilled promise for us since 1980. Tim Raines became the player Mookie was supposed to become but didn't. Mookie has never been a good leadoff hitter or a good clutch hitter. Mookie doesn't know how to take a pitch. Mookie strikes out all the time. This is how it's gonna end, isn't it?

C'mon Mookie! Don't swing at everything.

Y'know what would be great right now? A wild pitch. I'm always saying that and it never happens. But man, a wild pitch would score Mitchell and tie the game.

Oh shit! Mookie's gonna get hit! Wait! He jumped out of the way!

IT'S A WILD PITCH! OH MY GOD, THAT'S NEVER HAPPENED BEFORE! I ASKED FOR IT AND IT CAME!

WHERE'S MITCHELL? SCORE! SCORE!!!

He scored! He scored! Game tied! 5–5! We're not gonna lose! We're not gonna lose! Mitchell scored! And Knight's on second!

COME ON MOOKIE! COME ON!

* * *

If I heard what happened next from outside my own head, it sounded like this from my room, from the stereo, from Bob Murphy, over WHN:

And a ground ball trickling . . . it's a fair ball. It gets by Buckner!

* * *

This is what I know I heard, because this is what I screamed:

IT WENT THROUGH HIS LEGS!

IT WENT THROUGH HIS LEGS!

AAAGGGHHH!!!

AAAGGGHHH!!!

I DON'T FUCKING BELIEVE IT!

I DON'T FUCKING BELIEVE IT!

Boston Red Sox first baseman Bill Buckner leaves the field after his error on a ground ball hit by Mookie Wilson allowed Ray Knight to score the winning run for the New York Mets in the 10th inning of Game Six of the 1986 World Series. *AP Photo/Rusty Kennedy.*

AAAGGGHHH!!!

AAAGGGHHH!!!

* * *

Rounding third is Knight. The Mets win the ballgame! They win! They win!

* * *

If it was worth screaming twice, it was worth screaming more.

AAAGGGHHH!!!

IT WENT THROUGH HIS LEGS!!!

I DON'T FUCKING BELIEVE IT!!!

* * *

Gary Thorne chimed in:

Unbelievable, the Red Sox in stunned disbelief!

They weren't the only ones.

* * *

There were fourteen steps that separated upstairs from downstairs in our house, from where I was watching to where my parents were watching. While I was in the midst of my fifth (of fiftieth) AAAGGGHHH!!!, I leaped them in one furious bound. Well, not really, but it felt like it. I was downstairs in an instant. Dad couldn't believe it. Mom couldn't believe it. She believed enough in advance to videotape it, in case the Series should end in the tenth—though why we'd want to see it end in the tenth considering that would mean the Mets would have lost . . . oh, never mind—and kept telling me, "I

The New York Mets celebrate after rallying to defeat the Boston Red Sox, 6–5, in Game Six of the 1986 World Series. *AP Photo.*

taped it! I got it on tape!" Larry called. Larry, barely a fan most nights, was at a wedding and had to leave and listen in the car. He was calling me from his new "portable phone." I didn't know you could make calls from cars (Larry and his silly gadgets). He was heading over to ask me to explain how all this happened. My mother taped it, I said. You can see for yourself.

Because how the hell could *anyone* explain it?

CHAPTER 15

FROM THE CELLAR
TO THE PENTHOUSE

DAVE PERKIN

Bill Mazeroski's World Series-winning home run in 1960 joins Bobby Thomson's dramatics as one of the signature moments in baseball history.

As you read this account of Game Seven of the 1960 series, keep in mind the importance of the job of general manager in Major League Baseball. A GM places his fingerprints on all aspects of the baseball side of his organization: scouting, drafting, player development, and the major league team, referred to in industry circles as "The Big Club."

Modern GMs have an additional array of duties: free agent signings, trades, composition of the major league team, releasing players, hiring and firing managers and coaches, juggling enormous big league payrolls, legal issues, media interaction. In 2014, a GM's job is impossibly demanding and is often referred to as a 24/7/365 occupation.

Despite this relentless burden, the primary job of a GM in 2014 is the same as it was in 1960: assembling a major league roster that is capable of winning a World Series.

Ben Cherington, GM of the Boston Red Sox, performed a near miracle in 2013. In 2011, with a playoff berth nearly assured, the Sox suffered a late collapse and missed the postseason. A disastrous losing season followed in 2012. Wielding a deft touch, Cherington rebuilt the Red Sox and hired a new field manager, John Farrell, who led the club to the title.

Branch Rickey performed a similar feat over a half century ago with the Pirates. Pittsburgh had been the worst team in the NL in the early fifties. After losing a fight with Walter O'Malley for control of the Brooklyn Dodgers, Rickey was hired as Pittsburgh GM and set out to revamp the Bucs.

Savvy scouting brought prospects Dick Groat, Bill Mazeroski, Vern Law, and Roberto Clemente to Pittsburgh; brilliant trades provided other key contributors. A scant six years after suffering three consecutive 100-loss, last place seasons, the Pirates were World Champs.

As they do today, the Yankees of 1960 dealt from a position of strength. Their farm system was unequalled, providing key replacements as older stars faded. Trades—often with the unusually compliant Kansas City A's— brought necessary additions.

In his twelve years as Yankee Manager from 1949 through 1960, Casey Stengel guided New York to ten AL pennants and seven World Series titles. The true architect behind the Yankee success in this era was their GM, George Weiss.

Curmudgeonly and penurious, Weiss was an unparalleled judge of talent. His ability to recognize, sign, develop, and trade for top echelon players was stunning. After molding the Yankees into the premier dynasty in the history of the game, Weiss constructed the ballclub that became known as the 1969 "Miracle" New York Mets.

Never accused of being a "people" person, Weiss frequently developed adversarial relationships with his players, Billy Martin in particular. Weiss traded Martin to Kansas City after a 1957 nightclub fight in which witnesses claim Martin was not involved. Later, Weiss hired detectives to follow players he suspected of misbehaving on road trips.

Viewed from the perspective of scouting and player development, it is crucial to remember that behind every successful franchise is a capable GM. He serves as baseball's equivalent of an orchestra conductor, a maestro. This tenet was true in 1960; it is just as true in 2014.

Along with Game Six of the 1975 World Series, Game Seven of the 1960 World Series is considered the greatest game in baseball history.

October 2010

Unseen for fifty years, a film of the live TV broadcast of Bill Mazeroski's walk-off home run in the bottom of the ninth inning of Game Seven of the 1960 World Series was discovered late last year.

Recently transferred from film to DVD, the game broadcast will be shown on MLB Network in December. Major League Baseball has exclusive rights to the property, which will be made available for individual purchase by the public later this year. Originally, the film was shot in kinescope form—which simply means the live broadcast was filmed off a television monitor.

Mazeroski's Pittsburgh Pirates defeated the New York Yankees in that deciding game, 10–9. Despite getting outscored 55 to 27 in the series, the Bucs edged the Yanks to capture the title.

Considered one of the greatest games in baseball history, as well as a historical milestone, Game Seven of the 1960 Series has previously been preserved only in photographs and the official MLB World Series highlight film. No other recording of the game's TV broadcast—in whole or in part—is believed to exist.

To the delight of professional and amateur baseball historians, films of classic moments have randomly surfaced. In 1988, a grainy film was discovered of Game Three of the 1932 World Series, showing Babe Ruth's alleged "called shot." Earlier this year, MLB Network debuted by showing Don Larsen's perfect game in the 1956 World Series—another classic TV broadcast thought to be irretrievably lost.

The 1960 telecast was discovered in Bing Crosby's longtime Northern California home. Crosby, velvet-throated crooner and motion picture star, died in 1977 at the age of 74. A lifelong baseball fan, Crosby was a part owner of the Pirates for many years.

Reportedly, Crosby couldn't bear to watch the game on TV or in person, so he and his wife Kathryn headed to Paris. The Crosbys listened to the game with their friends Charles and Nonie de Limur.

"We were in this beautiful apartment, listening on shortwave, and when it got close Bing opened a bottle of scotch and was tapping it against the mantel," recalled Kathryn Crosby. "When Mazeroski hit the home run he tapped it hard; the scotch flew into the fireplace and started a conflagration. I was screaming and Nonie said, 'It's very nice to celebrate things, but couldn't we be more restrained?'"

Crosby hired a film company to make the kinescope, which he watched upon his return. The landmark film was then stored—unnoticed—in Crosby's Hillsborough, California, home for a half century. Robert Bader, VP of Bing Crosby Entertainment, found the film canisters while searching through the singer's personal memorabilia collection. The tins were innocently marked "1960 World Series."

I spoke to Nick Trotta, senior manager of library licensing for Major League Baseball. According to Trotta, the film—which had been stored in Crosby's wine cellar—was in pristine condition. Upon transfer, the resulting quality of the DVD is remarkable, given the film's age.

Manager Casey Stengel (left) and slugger Mickey Mantle of the 1960 American League champion New York Yankees. *AP Photo.*

First, a quick baseball history lesson. In 1960, major league baseball had only 16 teams—8 in each league. All clubs played a 154-game schedule. There were no divisions or layers of playoffs in 1960—the league champions advanced directly to the World Series.[1]

In the American League, the dynastic Yankees broke open a tight pennant race by winning their final 15 games. New York boasted a line-up full of All Stars and Hall of Famers, including Mickey Mantle, Whitey Ford, Roger Maris, Yogi Berra, Elston Howard, and Bill Skowron.

---

[1] The AL expanded to ten teams and a 162-game schedule in 1961, and the NL followed suit in 1962. Major League Baseball first introduced pre-World Series playoffs in 1969. Playoffs prior to that date occurred only after teams finished in a regular season tie. Those playoff games were counted as part of the regular season—in 1946, 1948, 1951, 1959, and 1962.

In the early fifties, Pittsburgh was one of the worst teams in baseball history. The Pirates had finished in last place (known as "the cellar" in baseball lingo) from 1952 through 1955. As the decade progressed, the Bucs improved their fortunes.

Their 1960 pennant was the organization's first in thirty-three years. Pittsburgh featured Cy Young Award winner Vernon Law, National League MVP and batting champion Dick Groat, budding superstar Roberto Clemente, and defensive stalwarts Bill Virdon and Mazeroski.

The Yankees blasted the Pirates in games two, three, and six by scores of 16–3, 10–0, and 12–0. Pittsburgh scored more modest wins in games one, four, and five by scores of 6–4, 3–2, and 5–2. The seventh and deciding game of the series was played at Forbes Field in Pittsburgh, on Thursday, October 13, 1960.

The contest was broadcast live across the nation via NBC-TV. At that time, all Series games were played in the daytime, never at night.[2]

Pirate play by play man Bob Prince handled the first half of the game solo, and legendary Yankee announcer Mel Allen covered the final innings.

The kinescope is in black and white despite the fact that the actual live broadcast was in color. NBC used a then-unusual technique that is now a common practice—a center field camera aimed over the pitcher's shoulder in toward home plate. Prior to 1960, most major league telecasts used a main camera positioned above and behind home plate, giving TV watchers a kind of "press box" view.

The Pirates, aided by a Rocky Nelson home run, jumped out to a 4–0 lead. New York, boosted by home runs from Bill Skowron and

---

[2] In 1960, all big league stadiums, with the exception of Wrigley Field, had lights. Tradition—quaint to some, outdated to others—dictated that Series games be played during the day. The first World Series night game occurred in 1971, thirty-six years after the first regular season night game.

Yogi Berra, rallied to take a 7–4 edge going into the bottom of the eighth. With a runner on and no outs, Bill Virdon rapped a certain double play ball at Yankee shortstop Tony Kubek. Suddenly, the ball took a bad hop and struck Kubek in the throat. Both runners were safe. Injured, Kubek was forced to leave the game. Pittsburgh, behind Hal Smith's home run, rallied to take a 9–7 lead.

After Virdon's ground ball, Casey Stengel can be seen ambling out of the Yankee dugout to check on Kubek. Allen stated that Smith's home run would be "remembered for a long time."

It was, until the top of the ninth. With the score 9–8 and runners on first and third and one out, Yogi Berra hit a ground ball down the first base line. Nelson, the Pirate first baseman, snagged the drive and toed the bag for the second out. That move by Nelson removed the force play on Mickey Mantle, the Yankee runner at first. Nelson needed only to tag Mantle to record the final out. The Mick wriggled away from Nelson's attempted tag and safely returned to first as the tying run scored.

Allen very succinctly explained the unusual play to viewers, while Mantle stood on first with his hands on his hips, looking calm and confident. Tied 9–9, the game moved into the bottom of the ninth.

Mazeroski led off for the Pirates. He took Ralph Terry's first pitch for a ball. After that pitch, Yankee catcher Johnny Blanchard jogged to the mound for a quick chat with Terry. With Blanchard back behind the plate, the center field camera was zeroed in on the action as Terry went into a full windup.

Mazeroski swung at Terry's offering and sent a long drive toward the 406-foot sign in left center. Yogi Berra, playing in left for the Yanks, drifted back as if he had a play on the ball. Quickly realizing his only chance was to play a possible carom, Berra reversed course and headed back toward the infield. No matter.

Bill Mazeroski rounds third base following his game-winning home run against the New York Yankees to win the 1960 World Series for the Pittsburgh Pirates. *AP Photo.*

Mazeroski's drive cleared the left-field fence, winning the game and the Series for Pittsburgh. To this day, it remains the only walk-off home run to win the seventh game of a World Series.

Allen can be heard describing the moment perfectly: "There's a drive to deep left field . . . look out now . . . that ball is going, going, gone! The World Series is over!"

After the ball cleared the fence, a camera located on the third base side captured a tight shot of Mazeroski's reaction. He bounced up and down, pinwheeling his arms in celebration as he held his batting helmet in his right hand. A mob of fans and teammates greeted Mazeroski at home plate.

The Yankees, somber in defeat, marched from their third base dugout. The tunnel to the visiting dressing room at Forbes Field was located next to the Pirates' first base dugout. This forced the Yankees to awkwardly walk around the delirious mob at home plate to get to their clubhouse.

Bob Prince, wearing a loud checkered sport coat, conducted a string of interviews in the clubhouse after the game. He then tossed the show back to Allen in the press box, who did a brief wrap-up and sign-off, ending the telecast.

Viewing the game film today exposes both subtle and obvious differences that have evolved in the game of baseball and the televising of baseball in the past fifty years:

- Not a single hitter wore a batting glove.
- Batting helmets were a fairly new invention in 1960, but no helmet had ear flaps.
- All uniforms, of course, were made of flannel.
- Plain black spikes, with no flashy corporate logos, were worn by all ballplayers.
- The seventh game in 1960 was played in bright sunshine, but I detected no eye black being used by any player.
- Baseball in 1960 was played at a much quicker pace than today. Pirates pitchers Vern Law and Elroy Face worked very rapidly and would probably draw "quick pitch" warnings in 2014.
- Hitters did not wander and dawdle outside the batter's box in 1960. Today, even a fine player like Dustin Pedroia exits the box after every pitch, seeming to suffer a nervous breakdown as he endlessly fiddles with his batting gloves.

Game Seven of the 1960 World Series was played in 2 hours and 36 minutes. This despite all the pitching changes, runs scored, and Kubek's injury. Postseason games today average between 3.5 and 4 hours. Average game time in the 1957 Series was two hours and twenty-seven minutes. The fourth and final game of the 1963 Series took 1 hour and 50 minutes. If the commissioner wants to learn why baseball has trouble attracting young fans, perhaps he should start studying postseason game times.

The Forbes Field crowd was particularly interesting. Almost every adult male wore a suit and tie. All six umpires wore suits and ties. One fan can be heard constantly chirping encouragement to his Pirates: "Just a little bingle!" he is heard saying during a Buc rally, and "Let's get two!" as Elroy Face faces a New York rally in the ninth. Prior to Mazeroski's homer, he can be heard advising, "Just get on Billy! We'll figure out a way to get you around!"

Little quirks were fascinating. Ballparks fifty years ago had unusually large mound circles, much larger than today. The check swing rule was not in effect. Several hitters took half swings that unquestionably would be called strikes today. Catchers and home plate umpires did not check with first or third base umps to confirm half swing strikes in 1960.

In the bottom of the eighth, Hal Smith faced a two-strike count. He took a half swing on a high fastball that undoubtedly would be called a strikeout today. In 1960, there was no strike call, not even an appeal. Smith homered on the next pitch.

During one of his frequent mound visits, Stengel chats with his pitcher while standing on the mound. He then descends off the mound onto the grass, turns, and walks back onto the hill to render some more advice. In 2014, Stengel's actions would be ruled to be a second mound visit, and the pitcher would be forced to leave the game.

From studying the telecast, my guess is that NBC used only four cameras: Center field, press box, first base, third base. Not a single play in the contest—critical or trivial—could be viewed a second time, as there was no instant replay. If a viewer missed the play, tough luck.

Replay was first used during a college football telecast in 1963. In 1960, TV viewers were not bombarded with blaring music, endless high-tech graphics, needless intrusions, promotional cutaways, or smart-aleck commentators. The only graphics used displayed a hitter's name across the bottom of the screen as he came up to bat.

Perhaps the best postscript to the classic game involves comedian Lenny Bruce. A friend of sportswriter Dick Schaap, Bruce attended the seventh game as Schaap's guest. It was the first and only game Bruce saw in person.

Bruce was stunned. "Geez, that was incredible," gushed the comic. "Are all baseball games like that?"

Shortly after the 1960 World Series, the New York Yankees fired Casey Stengel and George Weiss.

CHAPTER 16

JIM BOUTON MAKES A COMEBACK

LEW FREEDMAN

More famous for being funny in print because of his classic baseball book *Ball Four*, Jim Bouton discovered a way to resuscitate his pitching career after he lost a few miles per hour on his fastball: throw the knuckleball.

It may be argued after reading Bouton's prose that he was one of the funniest men in baseball history and that, although his Major League pitching career was rather compressed, he did perform excellent work for the New York Yankees in the early 1960s when he relied on a fastball and curve to get the job done.

Bouton was born in Newark, New Jersey, in 1939 and played college baseball at Western Michigan University before signing with the Yankees' organization at a time when they were still supervised by Casey Stengel in the dugout and identified with Mickey Mantle, Roger Maris, and Whitey Ford on the diamond.

A rookie at twenty-three in 1962, Bouton joined a Yankees rotation that still kept the team at the top of the American League. He finished 7–7 with a 3.99 earned run average for a club that won the pennant and bested the San Francisco Giants in the World Series. New York, by then under manager Ralph Houk, won in seven games, though Bouton did not appear in the Series.

The next year, 1963, was Bouton's coming-out party. He finished 21–7—the best of his career—with a 2.53 ERA and was chosen for the All-Star game as the Yankees again won the pennant. Indeed, Bouton appeared to be the next big thing on the mound for the Yankees, winning 11 games by the All-Star break. He was a traditional pitcher at the time, meaning that his collection of pitches featured the usual stuff.

"I throw the ball hard and I throw a curveball," Bouton said at the time. The curve was his outstanding specialty pitch, ranked amongst the best in the league. "I've got great confidence in it and I use it a lot in the pinch. I think that's one of the big reasons I've got off to such a nice start this year."

Unlike many of those who succeed at the top level of the sport, Bouton was a late bloomer. He said even in high school that he had trouble convincing the coach to use him in games because of his lack of speed and effectiveness. Because of that slow-motion beginning to his pitching career, Bouton experimented with trick pitches of every kind. That explains why, even as a twelve-year-old, he taught himself the knuckleball.

Bouton called his knuckler an early-career "necessity. I was so small I couldn't throw the ordinary stuff up to the plate hard enough to get anybody out. So I decided to throw the knuckleball. I read all about the knuckler in stories about Hoyt Wilhelm. He was with the Giants then. He was my big idol. It worked good, too. And I could get it over the plate."

Actually, much later, Bouton offered a revised version of his knuckleball beginnings, noting that he was first introduced to the knuckler while eating breakfast one day.

"I was ten years old and I looked at the cereal box," Bouton said. "It had a picture of Dutch Leonard on it and he showed you how to grip the knuckler. You should throw it with your fingertips, I learned. I ran out into the yard with my brother Bob and tried it. It was almost impossible to throw a ball without spin. I couldn't make it not spin. It took half a summer until I threw one accidentally. The ball was absolutely dead in the air. It broke and hit Bob in the knee. He was writhing in pain on the ground. I thought, 'What a great pitch.' I spent the rest of the summer trying to maim my brother and my father."

This doesn't mean that Wilhelm wasn't Bouton's idol—he served that purpose for many a knuckler and knuckleball wannabe over the years. But Bouton did a lot of the early work himself.

One way that Bouton developed his knuckler was through a hustle. Not hustling as in "working hard," but hustling as in "pool playing" or the like. He had a friend who admired his skill with the knuckler, and together they hatched a scam in junior high. His friend would approach somebody at school or in a playground who didn't know Bouton.

"There was always a new guy," Bouton said.

Bouton's friend would say, "See that little kid over there? I bet you if he throws you five pitches you won't be able to catch the ball."

The stakes were $1 and of course Bouton threw the knuckler, which danced all over the place in ways the sucker had never seen before.

"It would hit him in the chest or the forehead," Bouton said.

Bouton and his friend won their $1, which was decent money for such a limited work investment in the early 1950s. Then the newly won-over pigeon would recruit another youngster to fool and maybe the stakes would grow to $5.

"I had a good knuckler for a thirteen-year-old," Bouton said. "The problem with the knuckleball as a Major League pitcher is it's a long story. You usually come to it as a failure. I had a very good overhand curve and I had good control and then I had the knuckleball."

Bouton's high school in North Jersey was a large one with 2,500 students, many of whom were good athletes in all sports. Bouton was pretty well known, but then his father changed jobs and moved the family to the Chicago area. Bouton did not immediately win the confidence of the baseball coach, frequently warming up in the bullpen, but then not being used.

"My nickname was 'Warm-up Bouton,'" he said.

Bouton loved the sport and felt he was better than he had been able to demonstrate with his high school team. The summer after his junior year he joined an American Legion team.

"I was depressed," he said. "This was my last chance in baseball, really."

Trying to impress the coach, he worked extra hard. On a muddy, rainy day he was raking the infield to smooth it and was asked what he was doing. It was suggested that he play second base, but Bouton said he was a pitcher. He heard the coach say he had five guys better than he, but in the second game of the doubleheader, in the rain, he got his chance.

"It was the greatest moment of my life," Bouton said. "I found myself."

Instead of being a bench-warmer as a senior, Bouton won the respect of his coach. The coach, Jacob Eit, someone Bouton describes as "a very nice man," saw the benefits of Bouton's Legion play. "You had a great summer, son," Eit told him entering the school season of 1957. That year Bouton pitched a no-hit shutout in the state tournament, and he used the knuckler as an out pitch when needed.

"I had a knuckleball as squishy as a tomato," he said. "It turned out that even though I had good stuff, I had a knuckleball available. I was not going to give in. I was not going to abandon it."

However, in a sense he did so for a while. His fastball and curve got him signed by the New York Yankees.

"Basically, in the early 1960s I had good, conventional stuff," Bouton said. "I didn't throw a knuckleball in the minor leagues."

As Bouton matured into a six-foot-tall, 180-pound thrower (from the 150 he weighed while playing in Class D), his immediate need for the knuckler diminished. But in his own mind he was still a little guy and he did not want to completely discard this previous savior pitch, although the Yankees told him to do so.

"They didn't want me to become a guy with a trick pitch at my age," Bouton said. "I go along with that, but that doesn't mean I still can't throw a pretty good knuckleball. I practice it on the sidelines on days I'm not pitching. The way I look at it is that it's never going to do any harm to keep practicing the pitch. One of these days, when my hard one isn't quite so hard, the knuckleball may be the pitch to keep me employed a few years more."

That was as prophetic a prediction as any young hurler ever made about his own career without being able to literally look into the future. In the meantime, though, the knuckler was pretty much shelved as Bouton set down opposing batters. He did not overpower them, and somewhere along the way one of his catchers, either Yogi Berra or Elston Howard (Bouton can't remember which), bestowed the nickname "Bulldog" on him because he worked so hard to get outs.

Actually, for an additional pitch Bouton detoured into the slider, which worked well for him alongside that fastball and curve. In 1964, Bouton finished 18–13 with a 3.02 ERA and led the American League in starts with 37. New York was swept by the Los Angeles Dodgers in the Series, and Bouton lost Game 3.

Bouton demonstrated intelligence on the mound, and his teammates respected his efforts and savvy. "He's just a bear-down guy," Howard said. "He's at his best when he's behind on the count and there are men on base. When it's like that, he's just a bulldog—a battling kind of bulldog."

Yankee infielder Phil Linz, who also had been a teammate of Bouton's in the minors, said the pitcher was always thinking ahead about how to become better, even when he was young and out of the Major League limelight.

"There were the losing types and the winning types," Linz said that Bouton postulated. "He said you had to train yourself to think like a winner and he's done that."

When Bouton had a son that year, he started calling young Mike "Little Bulldog," because he wanted the boy to know that "he's got to battle and scratch for the extra comforts of life."

That season one of Bouton's trademarks, à la Willie Mays, was that his baseball cap flew off his head when he was trying to make a play. In Bouton's case it occurred when he bore down and fired a fast one. The cap taking off of its own accord like a plane from nearby LaGuardia Airport was a common-enough occurrence that it was remarked upon regularly by teammates and sportswriters.

First baseman Joe Pepitone urged Bouton to more or less nail the hat on his head, to "go ahead and hitch the cap on his dome with [thumb] tacks." Bouton said, "I think I'll nail up a suggestion box in the clubhouse." Nobody cares too much if your cap flies to the moon if you are winning about 20 games a year.

Hall of Famer Mays's cap tended to blow off in the breeze when he was chasing a fly ball full out or running the bases. Bouton said if he was employing his pitching form properly, his right arm brushed the bill of the cap right off his head. That was when he was throwing fastballs. The issue became a moot point later when he counted on knucklers. By the end of the 1964 season, Bouton had not thrown a knuckleball in a game for the Yankees in three years. He had no way of anticipating how that would soon change.

* * *

Although Bouton made his mark by winning 39 games in two seasons, he did not see far enough into the future when he was riding high to recognize that he would never again be as valuable a member of a big-league rotation. Those gaudy early statistics quickly became memories. In 1965, incurring a sore arm, Bouton went 4–15 with a 4.82 earned run average for the Yankees. In 1966, he finished 3–8, although his ERA was a much better 2.69. He made it into just 24 games, though. In 1967, appearing in only 17 games, Bouton went 1–0 but had become a reliever by then, throwing in just 44 1/3 innings. It looked as if his career was doomed and he would never again be a healthy pitcher.

"My arm was dead," Bouton said. "I didn't have a sore arm. When I finished 4–15, looking back I should have rested, but I wanted the ball. I got sent to the minors [in the 1960s] and that's when I realized, 'I'm never going to have that fastball again.'"

And he didn't. Bouton's velocity was gone, never to return.

"I went back to my high school knuckleball," Bouton said. He also said if he did not have the knuckler education to that point he never would have been able to pitch in the majors again, as it would have taken too long for him to adapt. "It would have been too late to learn it then. I got two more years in the big leagues. I couldn't have begun

Jim Bouton with the New York Yankees in 1967. *AP Photo.*

to learn the knuckleball at the age of thirty. Finally, it started to come for me."

In 1968, the Yankees gave up on Bouton and sold him away to a team that did not yet exist . . . except on paper. He emerged at the beginning of the 1969 season as a member of the Seattle Pilots expansion team in the American League. The Pilots lasted for just one year at Sicks' Stadium and then bolted for Milwaukee to become the Brewers. Feeling cheated by organized baseball, Seattle residents protested loudly and eventually landed the Mariners in 1977.

It's possible that if it were not for the presence of Jim Bouton and his energetic pen on the roster, no one would remember the Pilots except those who played on the team. Bouton, who finished the '69 season with the Houston Astros, spent the bulk of the year with the Pilots. As a side job he chronicled in a diary the comings and goings of the expansion team. Bouton's was the first truly candid, inside story of a team's happenings in a clubhouse and off the field, and he was mightily resented for telling tales that many felt should have been left private.

The book was wildly humorous and became a best seller and launched Bouton into a writing career after he retired from the game. It was a more innocent time, and halfway through the 2010s decade in another century many of the incidents that produced outrage seem tame. But the book will still make any fan laugh, as will Bouton's follow-up volumes.

Bouton's editor on *Ball Four* was one-time *New York Post* sportswriter Leonard Shecter, who in his foreword wrote that Bouton's original manuscript ran to 1,500 pages and Shecter's toughest challenge was leaving out so many funny things in compressing it.

It should be noted that the knuckleball plays a part in the first paragraph of Bouton's introduction. He wrote: "I'm thirty years old and I have these dreams. I dream my knuckleball is jumping around like a Ping-Pong ball in the wind and I pitch a two-hit shutout against my old team, the New York Yankees, single home the winning run in the ninth inning, and when the game is over, take a big bow on the mound in Yankee Stadium with 60,000 people cheering wildly. After the game reporters crowd around my locker asking me to explain exactly how I did it. I don't mind telling them."

Things never got that good with the Pilots, who finished 64–98. Bouton appeared in 57 games, all but one in relief, went 2–1, and compiled a 3.91 ERA. He did not get along very well with manager Joe Schultz, whose big-league playing career dated to 1939 and big-league coaching career dated to 1949. In *Ball Four*, Schultz was the butt of many jokes and humorous comments. He was conservative and Bouton was not.

Throwing the knuckler was one way in which Bouton was not conservative. It was all he had to work with by then, but he quickly learned that managers in general become very conservative around knuckleballers.

"They don't appreciate the pitch," Bouton said. "First of all, it looks strange. They're not thrown fast. It's hard to control the knuckleball. You can walk three or four guys. There was always the thought among managers that the knuckleball was sort of a free pass. They could understand a single or a double, but not the walks. The batter had to work for that [a hit]. That was OK."

It might be said that Bouton was a knuckleballer waiting to happen; that there was a certain inevitability that he one day would become connected to it in the majors. He had that kind of image, a player with a few quirks who could identify with a pitch with more than a few quirks. Anyone who throws a knuckler must have a sense of humor, and Bouton was renowned for that aspect of his personality.

He once said of the knuckleball: "It's a wonderful pitch. It defies logic. It flutters up there at grandma speed and renders strong men helpless."

The Seattle Pilots were a blip on the Major League radar screen, and Bouton didn't even last in Seattle as long (or as short) as the team. In all, Bouton pitched 122 2/3 innings and finished 2–3. Two of the 73 appearances were starts. Not being on the manager's favorite people list may have resulted in Bouton's exile and may not have been very surprising.

In late August of that season, Bouton was traded to the Astros for Dooley Womack and Roric Harrison.

"The Seattle Pilots traded me to the Astros for a bag of batting practice balls," is how Bouton analyzed that exchange.

The trade must have been consummated overnight because Bouton got the word he was on the go early in the morning with a hotel room phone call on a road trip to Baltimore. Since the Astros were only two-and-a-half games out of first place, he was happy to move to a better team. As he recounted in *Ball Four*, however, his roommate, Steve Hovley, seemed to think it was all a dream and then protested that he could not join the Astros on the road in St. Louis that day because he had a prior engagement at the Museum of Art with him.

"You promised," Hovley said.

When Bouton made his introductory phone call to Houston general manager Spec Richardson, he asked if the team had any receivers with knuckleball experience. Richardson said Johnny Edwards would give it a try. As has just about every knuckleball thrower, the time came in Bouton's career when he met up with a catcher who had no experience catching the dancing pitch, and in Bouton's case that guy was Edwards in Houston.

"He never caught the knuckleball before," Bouton recalled years later. "He would curse the ball. He didn't have the big glove."

Ball Four was a sensation when it came out in 1970, and one reason for it was what it revealed about ballplayers as human beings rather than as esteemed athletes. In one passage set in the locker room, Bouton watched fellow pitcher George Brunet get dressed. He noted the lack of undershorts being pulled on and asked Brunet if it was an oversight.

"No, I never wear undershorts," Brunet was quoted as saying. "Hell, the only time you need them is if you get into a car wreck. Besides, this way I don't have to worry about losing them."

Mothers always used to say you should wear underwear so you would not be embarrassed in that fictional car wreck, but how many guys have ever worried about losing their underwear?

Then there was the time that pitcher Marty Pattin had a bad game and left the field steaming hot. He kicked over garbage cans and hit the clubhouse door hard on his way in. Bouton and teammate Fred Talbot asked him what he was going to do if he had another bad game. Before that contest they put a hangman's noose in Pattin's locker. Cold. Lucky for all concerned, Pattin pitched well.

After the final month cameo in 1969, Bouton went 4–6 with the Astros in 1970, but *Ball Four* came out, creating massive attention and distractions, and Houston sent him to the minors. He was only thirty-one and still hoped to work his way back to the majors. Sitting in his hotel room, he fielded a telephone call from WABC-TV in New York. The book's humor, style, and the attention it received persuaded the station that he might make a good sportscaster. Bouton was tempted by the offer but turned it down.

"I said, 'No, I'm still pitching.' Two weeks later something changed my mind."

Bouton embarked on a new career as a sportscaster in New York, one that took him to two networks. He also appeared in some movies and TV shows and lectured widely, telling stories from *Ball Four*. Then he got the itch to pitch again. In 1975, Bouton signed a deal with the Portland Mavericks, a Class A team. He recorded a 5–1 record throwing the knuckler but dropped pitching again when he was summoned to help make a TV series out of *Ball Four* and act in it. The TV show was ill-fated, lasting only a handful of episodes.

At the time, the show was billed as a comedy where the action took place in the locker room rather than on the ball field. It wasn't about the games. The half-hour show had Bouton playing a relief pitcher named Jim Barton trying to hang on in the majors—which sounded transparently true to life in paralleling Bouton's own story. Apparently more people laughed at the book than the TV show.

Proving that a knuckleballer's arm never dies, Bouton made a comeback to baseball, his limber right arm showing enough life to gain him a contract with Chicago White Sox owner Bill Veeck, whose life was more emblematic of being a maverick than the Portland team's nickname. Bouton pitched a little for a White Sox minor-league team with little success but then played in the Mexican League, essentially the equivalent of AAA ball.

After still another minor-league stint in the Southern League at age thirty-nine, Bouton returned to the majors with the Atlanta Braves and went 1–3 in five starts. The knuckleball allowed him to reach the big leagues again.

"It was just a challenge," Bouton said of why he embarked on a second pitching career.

Bouton left the majors after the 1978 season, but he basically has never truly retired again. His final Major League stats included a 62–63 win-loss record and a 3.57 ERA. When sportswriters check in with Bouton periodically, they learn he is not exactly reclining on a couch somewhere, but is still pitching, throwing the knuckler in semipro senior leagues here and there around the Northeast. The *New York Daily News* sought him out in Massachusetts in 1995 when he was fifty-six. He was pitching then. In the spring of 2014, recently having turned seventy-five, he was still pitching.

"I threw this morning," he said to an interviewer in May of that year. "I try to throw 100 pitches every other day. I pitch amateur baseball, senior baseball. The younger guys think they are going to knock it

Jim Bouton wrote in his groundbreaking book, *Ball Four*, "You see, you spend a good piece of your life gripping a baseball, and in the end it turns out that it was the other way around all the time." *Michael E. Rodriguez, courtesy of iStock.com.*

out of the park. They swing from their asses and they pop it up. I have a lot of fun."

Bouton has this theory that every high school baseball pitcher should be required to learn how to throw the knuckleball, partially as a challenge, partially as an emergency back-up system, partially so they can see how the other half lives who can't throw a ball 95 mph.